Charles Cole Hine

The Agent's Hand Book of Insurance Law

(Fire Insurance)

Charles Cole Hine

The Agent's Hand Book of Insurance Law
(Fire Insurance)

ISBN/EAN: 9783337232665

Printed in Europe, USA, Canada, Australia, Japan

Cover: Foto ©Suzi / pixelio.de

More available books at **www.hansebooks.com**

THE

AGENT'S

HAND BOOK

OF

INSURANCE LAW.

(FIRE INSURANCE.)

HINE & NICHOLS.

———

NEW YORK:

THE INSURANCE MONITOR.

———

1887.

THIS BOOK

Is intended simply as a legal guide to the agent. It aims to place clearly before him those principles which apply to his every-day work, so as to enable him intelligently to perform his duties as a representative of the company, and guard against those things which in the past have involved companies, agents, and policy-holders in loss and trouble. It does not assume to cover the whole field of insurance law. It is not written for the lawyer, nor is it designed like the ordinary text-book to be cited as an authority in the courts, or in determining the rights of parties when once a controversy has arisen. The principle adopted in its preparation has been to treat those matters which are likely to involve the agent or his company in difficulty as things to be avoided, even though the weight of authority might in some cases sustain their legality. It seeks to indicate the safe channel rather than the edges of the shoals.

Special attention is given to those matters of practical importance which constantly come up between agent and company, agent and policy-holder, etc., while things not relevant to the agent's immediate work are not elaborated. It will fill a place not heretofore occupied, but a place which confessedly needs to be filled in the interest of the companies and their agency representatives. The authorities cited are, as a rule, the more recent decisions of the courts.

CHARLES C. HINE.
WALTER S. NICHOLS.

THE AGENT;

HIS RELATIONS AND RESPONSIBILITIES.

His Relations to his Principal.

The legal relations of principal and agent are the same in insurance as in other branches of business, except as they are modified by the special features of this particular occupation.

The commission given to the agent by his principal is the fountain from whence he derives all his authority, this and such written or verbal instructions as he may from time to time receive, fix the limits within which he is at liberty to act. They are his charter and by-laws. The moment he steps beyond them he ceases to act as agent or to represent his principal except to such as might be deceived concerning the facts. He becomes a mere wrong-doer and is liable to his principal for any injury that may result.

Paley on Agency by Lloyd, 9, 10, 16, 17 ; Ewell's Evans on Agency, 223, and cases there cited.

While insurance agents have not perhaps been prosecuted so often by their companies for violations of duty as have those engaged in some other branches of business, it is none the less true that the transgressing agent can always be held responsible by his company, and has been compelled in a number of cases to respond in damages.

In the case of Phœnix Ins. Co. vs. Pratt, decided by the Supreme Court of Wisconsin, Feb. 11, 1887, and reported in the 16th Ins. Law Journal, the agents had issued a policy on a certain mill which was afterwards found, on inspection by the special agent, to be a very undesirable risk. The local agents were thereupon instructed in writing to relieve the company of the risk "as soon as possible." Instead of doing so, they wrote requesting that it might run to expiration, which would occur a few days later ; that they disliked to cancel, and it would be a personal accommodation. Within four days, and before opportunity for a reply, the risk burned.

The company sued the agents for damages, alleging neglect to cancel as ordered. The Court ruled in favor of the company, using the following language : "They (the agents) were bound to the exercise of good faith and reasonable diligence in discharging the duties which they owed to their principal, and to make good any loss or damages arising from any negligent omission on their part in departing from the instructions of their superiors in the management of the company's business intrusted to them. * * * If the agents, from a mistaken view as to the safety of the risk and the wisdom of canceling it, or for any cause personal to themselves as agents of the company delayed acting, it was at their own peril."

The relation of the agent is what is legally termed fiduciary, that is, one of trust or confidence resembling that of a trusteeship. For this reason the law demands the utmost good faith, and jealously regards any conduct on his part savoring of disloyalty or abuse of power. The liabilities of the agent begin the moment he consents to act. He is presumed to be capable of performing the work which he undertakes, and is not excused for an injury resulting from incapacity or neglect. Where an agent undertakes to procure an insurance or is instructed to cancel a risk, and acts so negligently that loss results, he is liable for the consequences.

Wilkinson vs. Coverdale, 1 Esp., 74 ; Phœnix Ins. Co. vs. Frissell, 16 Ins. Law Jour., 75 ; also Phœnix Ins. Co. vs. Pratt, quoted above.

During the continuance of his agency he cannot represent any interest adverse to that of his principal. The agent has no legal right to accept a risk or a modification of the contract which he knows his principal would not approve, and can be legally compelled to surrender any profit he may gain from such a transaction.

7 Story's Eq. Jur., § 218, 309 ; Evans on Agency, 256.

All profits made in connection with his employment beyond such as are sanctioned by his principal belong to the principal. The agency cannot be surreptitiously used for personal advantage. If the agent agrees with the insured for a consideration to place the risk in a company which he represents, at a named rate of premium, or to waive any policy stipulation adverse to the applicant, the company may lawfully claim the consideration which he receives.

Evans on Agency, 243, and cases there cited ; Great Western Ins. Co. vs. Cunliffe, L. Rep., 9 Ch., 525.

The agent cannot bind his principal by any contract with himself without his principal's consent. Where, as a member of a firm, he has insured the firm's property with the consent of the general agent, he cannot by virtue of a mere understanding with the other members of the firm issue a renewal of the contract, which had expired, after a loss, on the ground of a verbal agreement for such renewal before the loss occurred.

Glens Falls Ins. Co. vs. Hopkins, 14 Ins. Law Jour., 317.

Another feature of this fiduciary relation of the agent is his obligation to account to his principal for the business of the agency. He cannot interpose the claims of third parties as a justification for withholding moneys in his hands, nor can he refuse or neglect to render an account-. ing when required. Such a refusal or continued neglect would be good ground for forfeiting his commissions.

Willard's Eq. Jur., 104.

The general rule is that in the absence of an understanding to the contrary the agent cannot delegate his authority to another in matters where his personal skill or discretionary powers are involved, unless it be to do a merely ministerial act. An agent who is authorized to contract insurances may delegate to his sub-agent the mere ministerial duty of notifying the applicant that the risk is accepted or upon what terms it is accepted, but he has no right to vest a sub-agent with any discretionary power of determining whether the risk will be accepted or upon what terms, unless his principal has assented to such a delegation.

Continental Life Ins. Co. vs. Willetts, 24 Mich., 268 ; Evans on Agency, 38.

In insurance, as in many other branches of business, the peculiar character of the work requires and contemplates the employment of sub-agents and clerks by agents who are commissioned by the company, but the powers granted to such subordinates must be kept strictly within the line of their necessary duties. The agent is liable to his principal for any abuse of power illegally granted to a sub-agent.

Cases frequently arise which were not contemplated or clearly provided for in the commission and instructions given to the agent. In all such cases the rule holds that the agent acts upon his own responsibility the moment he goes beyond the plainly defined line of his authority, and in case of damage resulting he can only be justified if it clearly appear that his course was such as good faith to his principal demanded. Where his authority is doubtful the same rule applies, he must act in good faith and be justified by the circumstances in his construction of his power. Where an agent is instructed generally to insure the cargo, and insures under a policy limiting the liability in case of loss, he will not be held responsible unless he violated his orders or was guilty of gross negligence or fraud.

Moore vs. Mourgue, 2 Cowp., 479 ; Boden vs. French, 10 C. B., 886.

Of course every specific grant of authority to an agent involves by implication whatever powers are usual or necessary for the purpose of executing that authority, and in the absence of specific instructions the general scope of his duties must aid in determining what authority he may exercise. An agent has an implied right to investigate concerning the origin of a suspicious fire, but he has no right as an agent to institute criminal proceedings. If his business is to deliver and countersign policies he has no right to waive proofs or adjust losses, and the insured is not justified in believing him to have such power.

Norman vs. Ins. Co., 4 Ins. Law Jour., 827; Bush vs. Ins. Co., 5 Ins. Law Jour., 207.

In the absence of anything to the contrary in the contract, the principal may at any time revoke the authority granted to the agent. If the contract between principal and agent gives a continued interest, which is rarely the case in fire insurance, the revocation of authority may give rise to proper claim for damages, but the authority to represent is ended nevertheless, and strangers must deal with the agent at their peril if notified. The principal is liable for labor and expense already properly incurred by his agent, but not for future gains which might have resulted had the agency been continued.

Shaw vs. Ins. Co., 49 N. Y., 681; Partridge vs. Ins. Co., 15 Wall., 458.

When the special work for which an agent has been delegated has been accomplished, his agency ends as of course, and when the power has been delegated to a firm it will terminate with the dissolution of the firm (unless it be joint and several) or death of a member.

Martine vs. Ins. Co., 62 Barb., 181; Guthrie vs. Armstrong, 5 B. and Ald., 628.

Such is the general doctrine concerning the relations subsisting between principals and agents, and this doctrine is rendered more emphatic by the peculiar and delicate nature of the responsibilities which must necessarily be delegated in insurance. It is indispensable to the success of the business, which must mainly be carried on at a distance from the principal office, that large discretionary powers must be granted to its representatives, and it is equally impossible for the companies to rigidly define the extent of those powers to the public with whom they deal. Hence it is that the agent, by ignoring or violating the limitations imposed on his authority, is in special danger of making his principal responsible for acts in excess of his authority where the party with whom he deals has a right to suppose that his acts are authorized. For, as between the company and the insured, the law will not inquire simply what was the actual authority possessed by the agent, but what was the authority which the party dealing with him had good reason to suppose he possessed. A large percentage of the disputes and litigations in which companies become involved is due to the acts of their representatives, unintentional, perhaps, but clearly in excess of their authority, while another large percentage is traceable to the ignorance of the agent concerning the legal effect of his acts. Hence it becomes important to consider the different classes of agency and the functions of each.

THE DIFFERENT KINDS OF INSURANCE AGENCY AND THEIR FUNCTIONS.

(a) THE BROKER.

In fire insurance two broad classes of agents exist—those who act for the insured and those who act for the company. Among the former is usually classed the broker. Strictly speaking, however, the broker is not exclusively the agent of either party. His functions are those of an intermediary to bring the two principals together. So long as he acts simply in that capacity he is not responsible to either party for a violation of the contract between them, but to whatever extent he acts in the interest of either he becomes the agent of that party.

Lycoming Ins. Co. vs. Ward, 8 Ins. Law Jour., 603 ; Mann vs. Meyer, 8 Ins. Law Jour., 905 ; Lycoming Ins. Co. vs. Rubin, 79 Ill., 402.

When, without any prior understanding on the part of a company or its agent, a broker bargains for insurance for his customer, he is exclusively the agent of the applicant in the work of securing the contract and all that relates to it. If his representations are false, or the premium has been paid into his hands, or he has been employed by the customer to secure a modification or cancellation of the policy, the latter is alone responsible.

Standard Oil Co. vs. Ins. Co., 5 Ins. Law Jour., 459; Story on Agency, § 134-5, 451-2 ; 35 Barb., 463.

But the moment he is intrusted by the company or its agents with the performance of any duty towards the company he becomes to that extent the agent of the company. If intrusted with a fully executed policy for delivery and collection of the premium under circumstances which justify the insured in believing that he is authorized to receive it in behalf of the company, a payment to the broker is payment to the company.

Lycoming Ins. Co. vs. Ward, ante ; Empire Ins. Co. vs. Mach. Co., 9 Ins. Law Jour., 399.

The mere payment of commissions according to a prevailing custom for such business as may be brought, will not of itself make the broker the company's representative. The delicate question of his relationship in each case must be determined by the specific circumstances. A party having desk-room in an agent's office and accustomed by a specific arrangement between them to bring business and share commissions, was intrusted by the agent with the duty of obtaining additional information regarding the risk, and it was held that the facts justified the doctrine that he acted for the company in securing it.

Mullin vs. Ins. Co., 15 Ins. Law Jour., 561.

A broker received from an agent of the insured and forwarded a risk to an agent in another State, who placed it and returned a fully executed contract, upon which the broker collected but retained the premium. The argument of the court was that the intrusting of such an instrument to one who must have been known to have been a mere broker in another State, was sufficient to justify the insured in regarding him as authorized by the company to receive it, and payment to him became payment to the company. But it was admitted that if the defalcation had been due to the original agent of the insured the case would have been different. A distinction was made between the relations of the two.

Universal Ins. Co. vs. Block, 15 Ins. Law Jour,, 219 ; Pottsville Ins. Co. vs. Improvement Co., 4 Out., 139.

The agency of the broker is at an end when the specific purpose for which he was employed has been accomplished. A broker employed merely for procuring insurance is not the agent of the insured for receiving notice of cancellation, or as regards any subsequent matter pertaining to the risk.

Von Wein vs. Ins. Co., 15 Ins. Law Jour., 158.

The safe rule for agents in all dealings with brokers or middle men is to regard them as vested with no authority by the insured beyond the mere placing of the risk, unless the contrary plainly appears.

(b) THE GENERAL AGENT.

The term general agent in insurance law is used to denote those who are commissioned with plenary power to act for the company in the transaction of certain departments of its business. But there is no magical power in the name to clothe with an authority greater than that which is formally conferred. Whatever be the title, the legitimate power of the agent is confined to that which is actually granted, and which varies all the way from a mere solicitor to one who has full authority to make and modify contracts and settle losses. His powers are usually limited by the equipments for his work. The possession of blank policies and renewal receipts duly signed are the usual insignia of the general agent ; and his authority, unless otherwise restricted, extends to the acceptance of risks, settlement of rates, and written conditions of insurance, in fact, to all matters pertaining to the making of insurance contracts which are consistent with the general character of the business. If not forbidden, he may waive the premium, consent to other insurance, and even modify the terms of the contract. He is frequently employed temporarily to adjust and settle losses as well as to receive notice and proofs.

Pechner vs. Ins. Co., 4 Ins. Law Jour., 782 ; Pitney vs. Ins. Co., 4 Ins. Law Jour., 765 ; Gloucester Mfg. Co. vs. Ins. Co., 5 Gray 498.

But it does not follow that such plenary powers are vested in an agent intrusted with blank contracts. The right to make a contract for another does not necessarily involve any rights regarding that contract after it has been made, and the power of the general agent is frequently more restricted regarding the contract after it has been made than before, by stipulations in the contract itself. The mere authority to make contracts of insurance does not imply any authority to adjust losses or to do other acts not connected with the granting of insurances.

Post vs. Ins. Co., 43 Barb., 351 ; Bush vs. Ins. Co., 63 N. Y., 531 ; Lohnes vs. Ins. Co., 6 Ins. Law Jour., 472.

An agent who is not specially authorized so to do has no right to cancel contracts already made, without the consent of his principal.

U. S. F. Ins. Co. vs. Tardy, 2 Ins. Law Jour., 60.

And generally the courts distinguish between the plenary powers granted to general agents in the making of contracts and their more restricted powers regarding such as are already complete. The authority of the agent, too, is restricted by the territorial limits of his jurisdiction. When he assumes to represent the company or to exercise authority beyond these limits, he is liable to the company as for any other unwarranted assumption of power.

(c) THE SPECIAL AGENT AND SOLICITOR.

The special agent is one who is intrusted with a particular duty under a limited authority. He can exercise no powers beyond those specifically intrusted to him and such as naturally flow from them. The duties of the solicitor are restricted to securing applications for insurance. Like the broker, he is a sort of middle man for bringing together the company and its customers; but, unlike the broker, he is the representative of the company for this purpose, and his obligations wholly lie in acting in its interest. The delivery of the policy when executed and the collection of the premium are also frequently added to his duties, and the possession of application blanks and of executed policies and renewals for delivery are the indices of his powers. It is his duty to see that the application is correctly understood and filled, and he is entitled to make all needed explanations for this purpose. He is bound to take note of any misstatement in the application regarding facts of which he has a personal knowledge, and he has no right to knowingly allow a misrepresentation concerning the risk to be made to the company, for the latter will often be held responsible for facts thus known to its agent. The neglect of these simple precautions has caused the defeat of the companies in many costly suits.

Planters' Ins. Co. vs. Myers, 7 Ins. Law Jour., and cases there cited ; Boetcher vs. Hawkeye Ins. Co., 8 Ins. Law Jour., 705 ; Kingston vs. Ins. Co., 42 Iowa, 46.

NOTE.—The language of the law and the language of the shop do not always agree. A GENERAL agent or manager, as understood in the craft, is one clothed with managerial and executive powers second only to those of the officers of a company, one to whom the local or resident agents of a State or of several States report, and from whom they receive their instructions ; but the LOCAL agent may be "General" in the sense employed in legal phraseology. A SPECIAL agent, as understood in the craft, is one who travels from the Head Office or General Agency clothed with supervisory powers, an expert who approves or cancels contracts, selects local agents, and otherwise represents the company officially or semi-officially ; but the solicitor or sub-agent (frequently the clerk or employé of the local, and wholly unknown to the company), is sometimes called "Special" in the language of the courts. If the legal and the professional nomenclature are both kept in mind, no confusion need arise from the terms herein used.

So in regard to the delivery of the policy and collection of the premium. Unless specially authorized no delivery should be made until satisfactory payment has been rendered, for the act of delivery will generally bind the company, and the agent is personally responsible for any failure to collect the premium.

Farmers' Ins. Co. vs. Mann, 9 Ins. Law Jour., 159 ; Critchett vs. Ins. Co., 9 Ins. Law Jour., 594; Rundle vs. Moore, 3 Johns., 36.

With the forwarding of the application or delivery of the contract and receipt of premium the work of the mere solicitor ends. He has no further powers regarding the insurance. He has no right to waive or modify any condition of the policy, consent to other insurance or increase of risk, nor do any other thing in relation to the contract unless specially authorized by the company. His knowledge concerning subsequent matters is not the knowledge of his principal, and the insured has no right to assume that he has such powers. He has no right to make a preliminary contract . for insurance.

Bush vs. Ins. Co., 5 Ins. Law Jour., 257 ; Morse vs. Ins. Co., 5 Ins. Law Jour., 409 ; Critchett vs. Ins. Co., 9 Ins. Law Jour., 594.

There is one important exception, however, to this rule. Where a renewal of the original contract is to be delivered, the agent should be careful that the conditions of the risk have not been materially changed within his knowledge, and that the representations in the original application are still true. For, by intrusting him with the delivery of a renewal the company is liable to be held responsible for changes of which he has received notice from the insured.

Whited vs. Ins. Co., 8 Ins. Law Jour., 368.

THE DOCTRINE OF WAIVER IN ITS RELATIONS TO THE AGENT.

No legal principle is fraught with more consequence to the companies in the conduct of agencies than that involved in the doctrine of waiver. If the express limitations to the agent's authority could always be brought home to the insured, or the agent himself were always strict and careful in the performance of his duty, waiver would be but little heard of in insurance. It arises from acts or conduct which are inconsistent with the strict terms of the contract itself. Whenever an agent, acting within the apparent scope of his authority, does that which will justify the insured in believing that some provision of the contract has been modified or expunged, his company may be made liable for the results. When the solicitor, in taking an application, knowingly consents to a false or incorrect statement of the facts regarding the title, character, exposure, or any other feature inquired about concerning a risk, and the applicant in good faith relies upon the agent, the responsibility for a misrepresentation which induces its acceptance by the company is imposed on the solicitor himself.

Wright vs. Ins. Co., 4 Ins. Law Jour., 251; Hadley vs. Ins. Co., 4 Ins. Law Jour., 611; Stone vs. Ins. Co., 15 Ins. Law Jour., 490; Donnelly vs. Ins. Co., 15 Ins. Law Jour., 698.

So if he delivers a fully executed policy and trusts for payment the contract will generally be binding, but he will be himself liable for the premium unless authorized to give credit.

Home Ins. Co. vs. Curtis, 5 Ins. Law Jour., 120; Washoe Co. vs. Ins. Co., 5 Ins. Law Jour., 773; Von Wein vs. Ins. Co., 15 Ins. Law Jour., 158.

So an agent who has power to contract by consenting or seeming to consent to a vacancy, alteration, increase of risk, other insurance, incumbrance, or any modification of a subsisting contract may deprive his company of its right to protection against such modifications, or by his conduct after a loss may mislead the insured and prevent the company from securing the evidence needed to determine its liability.

Home Ins. Co. vs. Warehouse Co., 6 Ins. Law Jour., 739; Lycoming Ins. Co. vs. Dunmore, 5 Ins. Law Jour., 93; Akin vs. Ins. Co., 6 Ins. Law Jour., 341.

But unless the insured has actually been misled or was justified in relying on the agent, he cannot escape the responsibility of his acts by charging the fault on the agent. He cannot justify an alienation because it was known to a mere local agent. He cannot claim to be insured on the strength of a verbal assurance to that effect by an agent who had no power to contract. He cannot claim any advantage in the settlement of his loss from the acts of an agent who had no authority to do more than countersign or deliver policies.

Bush vs. Ins. Co., 5 Ins. Law Jour., 257 ; Morse vs. Ins. Co., 5 Ins. Law Jour., 409 ; Home Ins. Co. vs. Lindsey, 5 Ins. Law Jour., 549.

The safe rule for the agent is to avoid all acts or conduct which are liable to mislead the applicant or the insured either as to his own authority or the company's requirements. Especially is this necessary on the occurrence of losses, where a peremptory denial of liability may release the claimant from the necessity of furnishing evidences required by the company, or a hasty assumption of liability and a corresponding course of conduct may prevent the interposition of defenses against an unrighteous claim. The application and the contract define in most cases the true course of procedure, which should be deviated from only when circumstances seem to demand it. In general an agent will best serve his company in doubtful cases by inaction, except in acquiring facts and insisting on the protection of property while awaiting instructions from headquarters. See "what to do in case of fire."

The Preliminary Negotiations and the Premium.

However limited may be the agent's authority, the fact that the representations in the application are the basis on which the contract is made by the company, renders it important that he should be familiar with the law of the contract itself. Justice to the applicant, who so often relies upon his advice and assistance, as well as to his company, demands that every element of information required for framing the contract should be free from ambiguity. As no contract is said to be complete until the minds of the parties are in accord on every essential point, so it may be added of the negotiations for insurance. They can be regarded as satisfactorily ended only when every pertinent question has been distinctly settled. When the application is by the terms of the policy made a part of itself or is distinctly referred to and relied on, an important error will either vitiate the whole insurance or make the agent responsible for a liability on the part of the company which is chargeable to his fault.

Rohrbach vs. Ins. Co., 4 Ins. Law Jour., 737 ; Continental Ins. Co. vs. Kasey, 4 Ins. Law Jour., 208.

Even when the application is not thus incorporated its statements are representations used to secure a contract, and if they are false in matters that are material they will vitiate the insurance unless the agent was at fault.

Ryan vs. Ins. Co., 8 Ins. Law Jour., 659; Byers vs. Ins. Co., 9 Ins. Law Jour., 743.

All applications should, if possible, be reduced to writing and duly signed by the applicant. Mere verbal understandings or policies procured on the agent's personal representations are not only open to all the inaccuracies, disputes, and misunderstandings which attend verbal arrangements of any kind, but they impose on the agent a responsibility which belongs entirely to the insured. The agent in such case is likely to find himself in the attitude of a sponsor for those whose risks he has secured. In case of a disputed loss his acts and conduct are the subject of contention between the parties and of criticism by the courts, while they may be condemned by both parties to the dispute, and an unrighteous loss may thereby be imposed upon his company.

City Ins. Co. vs. Bricker, 9 Ins. Law Jour., 784 ; Baile vs. Ins. Co., 10 Ins. Law Jour., 657.

Special care should be taken in all negotiations, against the use of language which is likely to convey an impression that the bargain is completed, especially when the agent has been intrusted with policy blanks. As a rule no insurance contract should be made complete until actually reduced to writing and the premium settled, and every negotiation should be terminated, if successful, by a clear understanding on the part of the applicant that the contract will begin with the delivery of the written instrument. In the case of Putnam vs. Ins. Co. (7 Ins. Law Jour., 550) the agent had, on account of the hazardous character of the risk, refrained from issuing the policy until the special agent should inspect the building; but though no premium had been paid he had justified the applicant in believing the contract was complete, and the company was compelled to pay the loss. In the case of Mann vs. Meyer (8 Ins. Law Jour., 905) and again in that of Revere Ins. Co. vs. Chamberlin (10 Ins. Law Jour., 397) the agents involved both themselves and their companies in trouble by orally agreeing for insurance, and then undertaking to issue a written contract after the fire had occurred, and where in one case the fact of the loss was kept concealed from the agent until the policy had been secured. It should be borne in mind that where an agent is authorized to contract the mere omission of the policy will not prevent a contract from being enforced if there has been a valid agreement ; a court of equity will compel the issue of a policy.

Franklin Ins. Co. vs. Taylor, 5 Ins. Law Jour., 671.

No negotiations for insurance are complete until the parties have agreed upon those things which are essential to enable a court to frame the contract. These are the subject-matter of the risk, the amount of indemnity, the commencement and duration of the risk, and the amount and terms of payment of the premium. It is not necessary that all of these should be specifically stated. Thus, the usual time of one year, the usual form of policy, and the usual terms of payment may all be presumed if there is nothing to the contrary. But any uncertainty regarding what property was to be covered, or for how much, or what premium would be charged, obviously could not be supplied, and a negotiation in which these points or any others of essential importance remained unsettled would be unfinished. The same is true where something further remains to be done or settled before contracting.

Eames vs. Ins. Co., 6 Ins. Law Jour., 689 ; Strohn vs. Ins. Co., 37 Wis., 625 ; Millville Mut. Ins. Co. vs. Collerd, 38 N. J., 480; Walker vs. Ins. Co., 8 Ins. Law Jour., 847.

Thus, in the case of Millville Mut. Ins. Co., just cited, the applicant held the policy under advisement, without paying the premium, while he investigated the standing of the company. This was held not to be a completed contract. So in the case of Walker, a note was given for the premium with the understanding that it was to be returned if the application was not accepted, and the contract was decided to be incomplete. The agent should be particularly guarded against allowing the insured to believe the agreement is complete until the premium has actually been settled ; for, if clothed with sufficient authority, he may otherwise by his conduct unintentionally waive its payment. All the terms of the insurance in like manner should conform to what the agent has reason to believe that the company will insist on, for a verbal contract if once completed becomes the real contract between the parties, and the insured can compel the company to comply with it in its written policy. But when the policy has once been accepted by the insured this will supersede the oral agreement unless the insured has in some way been misled or misrepresented by the agent.

Southern Ins. Co. vs. Yates, and cases there cited, 6 Ins. Law Jour., 394.

Where the agent has power to bind temporarily until the company can be consulted, as little as possible should be left to the memory. The *ad interim* receipt should state with sufficient fullness all the essential conditions of the insurance, and a recording agent should always bear in mind that actual payment of premium is not essential to the completion of an oral contract.

Davenport vs. Ins. Co., 17 Iowa, 276 ; Hamilton vs. Ins. Co., 5 Barr., Pa., 339.

Nor is it always essential that a thorough understanding should have been arrived at touching the conditions of insurance if these have been left to the agent's discretion. In Ellis vs. Ins. Co. (50 N. Y., 502) the selection of a company had been left to the agent, who unknown to the insured had made a selection; this completed the contract. In Ins. Co. vs. Taylor (5 Ins. Law Jour., 671) the agent rendered his company liable by leading the applicant to believe that the insurance was complete, when in fact his authority, in the class of risks involved, was limited to forwarding the application. The evidence being conflicting as to knowledge by the applicant. All applications should be promptly forwarded to the company and the result communicated to the applicant ; for, when he has been led to believe that this will be done, both the agent and his company may be liable for the consequences of unreasonable delay.

Walker vs. Ins. Co., 8 Ins. Law Jour., 847.

Even though the applicant personally fills and signs the blank, the agent is likely to be called on to explain the meaning of the terms, and his tacit assent to the language employed when he has reason to doubt its correctness may relieve the insured from responsibility for misstatements. Inadvertance or suppression of knowledge on the part of the agent when securing the application may deprive the company of its protection against false representations. Thus in Westchester Fire Ins. Co. vs. Earle (5 Ins. Law Jour., 61) the fact of an agent doing some act to mislead the insured, or remaining silent when he ought to have spoken, was adjudged sufficient to defeat a clause relating to other insurance ; and the same rule was again enforced in Kitchen vs. Hartford Ins. Co. (14 Ins. Law Jour., 594) where he was verbally informed of the facts at the time the application was filled. So in Van Schaick vs. Ins. Co. (68 N. Y., 434) and in Williams vs. Ins. Co. (12 Ins. Law Jour. 708) tacit knowledge concerning defective title by the agent bound his company. It is of the first importance, therefore, that the solicitor, as well as the recording agent, should understand the laws governing the specified features of the contract itself, which we shall shortly discuss from the agent's standpoint.

When the negotiations are conducted by correspondence it has been a matter of no little debate in the courts as to when a perfect agreement has been reached. By some it has been insisted that a proposition made on behalf of the insured is complete the moment an unconditional answer of acceptance has been mailed by the insurer. By others it has been held that the contract is only complete when the insured has received the notice of its acceptance. The former seems the better view, and is certainly safer for the guidance of the agent. No policy nor acceptance of any kind should be forwarded to a sub-agent for delivery unless the latter is at the same time granted a discretionary power to withhold the acceptance or the agent is prepared to close the contract on the spot. For the sub-agent by such an act, in the absence of discretionary power, is made a mere medium of communication, and the acceptance is beyond recall the moment it first passes from the agent's control.

Halleck vs. Ins. Co., 26 N. J., 268 ; Eames vs. Ins. Co., 6 Ins. Law Jour. 689 ; City Ins. Co. vs. Zoller, 4 Ins. Law Jour., 478.

For the same reason completed policies should not be sent to a solicitor without discretion as to their withholding ; for, even though they stipulate that they are not binding until the receipt of premium, it has been held that such a sending is practically a delivery to the insured, which will waive the condition as to payment.

Eames vs. Ins. Co., *supra.*

Again, in the delivery of the policy, the agent should never rely on such a clause for protection in case the premium is not at once paid ; for, as has been said, an unqualified delivery is a presumption that credit for the premium is intended.

Von Wein vs. Ins. Co., 15 Ins. Law Jour., 158 ; Eagan vs. Ins. Co., 6 Ins. Law Jour., 832 ; Bowman vs. Ins. Co., 5 Ins. Law Jour., 9.

Unless the agent is authorized and intends to give such credit, if the circumstances require a delivery of the policy, it should be made with a written stipulation that it shall only be in force upon actual payment. Unless the agent is authorized to give credit, he renders himself personally liable to his company by absolutely surrendering the policy or absolutely contracting in any way without first receiving the premium.

Paley on Agency by Lloyd, 9, 10, 16, 17 ; Ewell's Evans on Agency, 307.

So, if the agent charges himself with a premium that is not received, he assumes personal responsibility for a completed contract, and must look to the insured as to any other debtor for his re-imbursement. For the same reason, too, no agreement should be made with a broker by which the latter is charged with the premium, unless it is intended that the policy shall be binding and the broker alone responsible for the payment.

Bang vs. Ins. Co., 1 Hughes, 290 ; Wheeler vs. Ins. Co., 10 Ins. Law Jour., 354 ; Eagan vs. Ins. Co., 6 Ins. Law Jour., 832.

Caution should be used in accepting payment of premium where the question of contracting is referred to the decision of a higher authority. Such conditional acceptance will not make a binding contract, but in case of dispute it will be claimed as evidence in favor of a completed contract, and the agent's receipt should always show that the premium is to be returned unless the risk is accepted.

Walker vs. Ins. Co., 8 Ins. Law Jour., 847.

Adjustments of premium through personal accounts between the agent and the applicant should, so far as possible, be avoided. While the law permits an agent in good faith to agree with the applicant that payment may be made through the canceling of an obligation, or in some other form than cash, so long as the applicant has no reason to believe that a cash payment is essential, it does not look with favor on this mode of dealing, and absolutely forbids the utilizing of the agency in this way for the personal advantage of the agent against the interest of his principal. If the insured has reason to believe that such a method of settlement will not be acceptable to the company, much more if he knows that it is a fraud on the rights of the principal, it will not be sustained. In Hoffman vs. Ins. Co. (4 Ins. Law Jour., 398) an attempted settlement of premium was made through the barter of a horse, and the court declared that it was a fraud upon the company, that an agent can only bind his company by acts done in the usual line of his business.

Upton vs. Mills, 11 Cush., 586 ; Story's Agency, Sec. 60 and note ; 1 Pars. on Cont., 41, 42.

If an agent in the exercise of his discretion accepts a note for the premium, he must bear in mind that the failure to pay such a note when due will not, unless specially stipulated, affect the validity of the policy. Until the policy is canceled in the ordinary way the only remedy will be a suit on the note, and if the insured is not responsible he will secure his insurance for nothing.

Wilson vs. Ins. Co., 8 Ins. Law Jour., 880 ; Shakey vs. Ins. Co., 7 Ins. Law Jour., 223.

The acceptance of the application by an agent authorized to contract, or the entry by him of a brief memorandum describing the risk, when done with the intent to issue a policy, is sufficient, without some understanding to the contrary, to make a binding contract, and the agent in thus concluding the negotiations should be careful that his intention should be carefully understood, unless he regards the contract as actually in force.

Thus, in Franklin Ins. Co. vs. Taylor (5 Ins. Law Jour., 671) the agent who took the application did not inform the applicant that it must be forwarded for approval, but led him to believe that the assurance was complete, and his company was held to be liable. In Continental Ins. Co. vs. Jenkins (5 Ins. Law Jour., 514), on the other hand, there was a series of negotiations which resulted simply in an agreement as to the terms on which the applicant might insure, if he chose, and assurance by the agent that he would accept the terms when proffered. No proffer, however, was made until after the loss, and it was held that no valid contract had been made.

See also Patterson vs. Ins. Co., 5 Ins. Law Jour., 376; Taylor vs. Ins. Co., 8 Ins. Law Jour., 851; Stron vs. Ins. Co., 4 Ins. Law Jour., 680; Weeks vs. Ins. Co. 7 Ins. Law Jour., 552; Moody vs. Ins. Co., 9 Ins. Law Jour., 276.

FILLING IN THE POLICY OR APPLICATION.

Unless dictated or suggested by the agent, the language in the application is presumed to be that of the applicant, for which the company is not responsible. But with the policy the language used is, under all circumstances, that of the insurer, who is assumed by the courts to be expert in its use. The consequence is that any vagueness in the terms of the latter or anything indefinite in its language will be construed in a sense that is most favorable to the insured. Misrepresentations and palpable violations of policy conditions are likely to be excused by the courts if it can be shown from the wording of the policy that the insured might have had a reasonable doubt as to the misrepresentation or violation.

Miller vs. Ins. Co., 7 Ins. Law Jour., 378; West vs. Ins. Co., 5 Ins. Law Jour., 430; Rann vs. Ins. Co., 5 Ins. Law Jour., 515; Miller vs. Ins. Co., 7 Ins. Law Jour., 378.

This rule is particularly true of the written portions which are so often filled in by the agent. These are properly regarded as expressing the intentions of the insurer in each individual case, and any language used in them which may be inconsistent with the printed portions will override the latter.

Ætna Ins. Co. vs. Jackson, 13 B. Mon., 242; Benedict vs. Ins. Co., 31 N. Y., 389; Reynolds vs. Ins. Co., 47 N. Y., 597.

The same principles, of course, control the language of the application in so far as the agent is responsible for it. The selection of appropriate language therefore becomes in both cases of the utmost importance. No reliance should be placed on any previous understandings or verbal agreements. These will be entirely disregarded by a court if the written instrument can be interpreted without them. If, for instance, a policy be written on "tools," a verbal understanding that certain classes of tools were not included will have no effect. The only exception to this rule is where it clearly appears that a fraud has been perpetrated or that both parties intended something different.

Lovewell vs. Ins. Co., 7 Ins. Law Jour., 672; Southern Ins. Co. vs. Yates, 6 Ins. Law Jour., 394.

The first and most general rule regarding the choice of words in filling a policy or application is that, 'if possible, they should convey to the popular mind just what is intended ; for the first question that will be asked by a court is, not what the agent meant, but how would the insured naturally understand the language. If the idea is one which is naturally or necessarily embodied in technical terms, such terms should be chosen, if possible, as have a well-understood meaning either in the community or the particular branch of business in which the insured is engaged ; and in no case should technical words be employed which mean one thing with the underwriter and are liable to mean another to the insured. If words have more than one sense or meaning it should be borne in mind that the meaning most favorable to the insured, or which will give the largest indemnity, will usually be adopted by the court. While the meaning may not be distorted or stretched to embrace what was clearly not intended, whenever terms are employed which may fairly indicate an aggregate or collection of risks they will so be construed. Thus a factory may be interpreted as meaning a collection of buildings; a stock of dry-goods or groceries may include a great variety of articles which do not strictly belong to either line of trade ; household furniture may cover articles which, taken apart from the rest, are not ordinarily spoken of as furniture.

Germania Ins. Co. vs. Francis, 6 Ins. Law Jour., 235 ; Hewitt vs. Ins. Co., 10 Ins. Law Jour., 375 ; Houghton vs. Ins. Co., 10 Ins. Law Jour., 547 ; Harris vs. Ins. Co., 4 Ins. Law Jour., 799 ; Blake vs. Ins. Co., 12 Gray, 265 ; Peoria Ins. Co. vs. Lewis, 18 Ill., 562 ; Moadinger vs. Ins. Co., 2 Hall, 490.

In all cases of doubt the best practical guide for the agent is to regard the question from the standpoint of the insured, and judge whether the language is likely to be construed as including more than was intended. Technical words that have a fixed and thoroughly understood meaning in a particular business, and which are there universally used to express the idea intended, are usually the safest and best to use in such business. In Daniels vs. Ins. Co. (12 Cush., 430) the Court said : ''The general rule is that if any person or any company, foreign or domestic, shall engage in any department of business, they must be presumed to be acquainted with the rules and usages of such business, to be conversant with the language employed in it, whether strictly technical or not.

See also Houghton vs. Ins. Co., *supra*, and cases there cited.

But the agent should be on his guard not to confound this technical use of words with a frequent practice of employing them by many parties in a loose or modified sense. The courts never allow the claim of usage to override the ordinary meaning, unless the use is so general as to fix a special meaning.

Myers vs. Carl, 30 L. J., Q. B., 9—s. c., 7 Jur., N. S., 97.

Another danger to be specially guarded against in filling a policy is that of overriding its express stipulations by impliedly assuming a risk that is inconsistent with such stipulations. If the employment of a dangerous oil or the keeping of a dangerous explosive is a well-understood part and parcel of any trade or business, a risk taken on such a business will be assumed to permit a continued use or keeeping of the dangerous material in spite of a general prohibition to the contrary. Whenever it is desired to restrict any practice or usage that is common in connection with a risk, that intention should be made clear in the written portion of the policy.

Buchanan vs. Ins. Co., 4 Ins. Law Jour., 458 ; Bayly vs. Ins. Co., 4 Ins. Law Jour., 503 ; Carrigan vs. Ins. Co., 10 Ins. Law Jour., 606.

Not only should the agent be fairly conversant with the character of the particular trade or business, in order to intelligently write the policy, but he should thoroughly understand the legal import of the various terms commonly in use in the fire insurance contract, which we shall consider further along.

From what has been said, not only the great importance of well-chosen words will be seen, but also the importance of letting each party to the contract speak for himself. Where it is possible to avoid it, the agent should never fill up an application, that is the province of the applicant; and if he is sufficiently intelligent to do it correctly he should do it alone. It is difficult for a man to serve two masters, and in the case of an insurance agent he is in danger of being adjudged by the court to occupy a position exactly opposite from the one he intended, if he helps an applicant fill up an application.

Davenport vs. Peoria Ins. Co., 17 Iowa, 276 ; [Beebe vs. Hartford Ins. Co., 25 Conn., 51 ; Pierce vs. Nashua Ins. Co., 50 N. H., 297 ; Rowley vs. Empire Ins. Co., 36 N. Y., 550; 2 Parsons on Contracts, 535, 661, and notes ; Swan vs. Watertown Ins. Co., Pa. S. C., 10 Ins. Law Jour., 392.

WHO MAY BE INSURED.

The law allows an insurance to be effected by any party who has such an interest in the property that direct pecuniary injury is likely to result from its damage through fire; but that interest must be of an essentially legal character, not a mere expectancy. A man may be the expectant heir of a millionaire, but he has no right to insure the property of the latter unless he has some legal claim. A son has no right on account of his mere relationship to insure his father's property. On the other hand, a man living on mere sufferance on property, and caring for it under an agreement that it shall eventually become his, has been allowed to insure.

Baldwin vs. Ins. Co., 12 Ins. Law Jour., 371 ; Barracliffe vs. Ins. Co., 13 Ins. Law Jour., 190, and cases there cited ; Agricultural Ins. Co. vs. Montague, 7 Ins. Law Jour., 708.

So parties in temporary possession or control of property, under circumstances where they would be liable in case of loss or where they would be justified in acting for the owner, and those having liens of any kind where there is danger of a moneyed loss through its destruction, are allowed by the law to insure.

Harvey vs. Cherry, 7 Ins. Law Jour., 315 ; Babson vs. Ins. Co., 4 Ins. Law Jour., 50 ; Rohrbach vs. Ins. Co., 4 Ins. Law Jour., 737 ; Franklin Ins. Co. vs. Martin, 8 Ins. Law Jour., 134.

More than this, such parties need not state the nature of their interest at all, unless it is called for, and are often permitted to recover, not simply what they are shown to have lost, but what it is possible they may have been injured. Such being the laxity or liberality of the law, the temptations to fraud are obviously strong, and the companies for their own protection generally insist that the nature and extent of the applicant's interest shall be clearly stated. Any failure to do this through the remissness or blunder of the insured is likely to defeat his insurance, and, if through the fault of the agent, may involve both himself and his company in trouble. It by no means follows that an applicant should be granted insurance because the law will support a policy issued to him. On the contrary, policies should be restricted, as far as possible, to the principal parties in interest, or those having the actual title to the property; leaving the rights of others to be secured by proper indorsements regarding payment of the loss, or else should include as many interests as possible. Where it is necessary to separately insure subordinate interests their character should be closely scrutinized, and, whatever their title or interest, care should be taken that there shall be no temptation to fraud. The nature of these various interests will now be examined more in detail.

Martin vs. Ins. Co., 15 Ins. Law Jour., 371.

NOTE.—These details are given, not to enable an agent to practice upon them, but to warn him against them. A book of this character would be incomplete were these points omitted ; but the agent is urgently recommended to limit his writings to parties who are actual owners, and to decline all complicated cases until he has fully corresponded with his company, advised it of the nature of the case in hand in every detail, and received special authority to entertain the proposed risk. In this connection the agent is referred to other portions of this book wherein the limitations of his authority and his legal liabilities for exceeding that authority are treated. It is always safe to be on the safe side.

THE SUBJECT-MATTER OF INSURANCE.

BUILDINGS.

The term "building" signifies a single structure or edifice complete in itself, regardless of the uses to which it may be put. So "house," "barn," "shed," and the like are simply particular classes of buildings. But such words as "factory," "mill," and "store," having special reference to the business or occupation, have sometimes been allowed to include a number of collective buildings used for one general purpose.

Hews vs. Ins. Co., 8 Ins. Law Jour., 291 ; Brugger vs. Ins. Co., 8 Ins. Law Jour., 293 ; Bigler vs. Ins. Co., 20 Barb., 635.

For this reason the words "building," "house," and the like should be added when describing a risk which might otherwise be indefinite, as "mill building" or "building" used as a factory. A building includes whatever permanent attachments to the structure in the shape of fixtures go with the realty in case of sale and which are an integral part of the structure itself. Thus gas and water pipes, stationary tubs and basins, and the like, are an integral part of the building. So in some cases shafting and other fixed machinery, when manifestly necessary for the use for which the building was designed, have been treated by the courts as a part of the structure, the rule being, when the language is not clear, to seek the intention of the parties. For this reason care should be taken to except from a policy all such articles as are not intended to be included, but which might naturally be regarded as belonging to the structure. Church bells, clocks, and organs, shafting, belts, stationary engines, mirrors, or other ornaments so fastened that their removal would mar the appearance of the walls, when these are the property of the insured, should generally be excepted or else specifically included to avoid all controversy.

Brugger vs. Ins. Co., 8 Ins. Law Jour., 293 ; McKeage vs. Ins. Co., 9 Ins. Law Jour., 598 ; Liebenstein vs. Ins. Co., 9 Ins. Law Jour., 588.

The word "fixtures" in the sense in which it has just been used as denoting component parts of the building itself should seldom, if ever, be employed in the policy. Its use in insurance is restricted to such fixtures as are personal property, trade-fixtures as they are called, which a tenant is at liberty to remove from the building. When a building is fitted up for occupancy as a store or factory, for instance, certain *permanent* fittings may be added by the owner or by the tenant to adapt it to its purpose, these are part of the realty. There are others, such as counters and chandeliers, which, though actually fastened to the building by the tenant, are simply for his own use in his business, and which the law allows him to remove, and are the only proper subjects to be insured as trade-fixtures. The others are included in a risk on the building. If intended to be excluded it is safer to say so.

Whitemarsh vs. Ins. Co., 16 Gray, 369 ; Brugger vs. Ins. Co., and McKeage vs. Ins. Co., *supra.*

A building or house will usually include such wings or additions as are naturally a part of it.

Blake vs. Ins. Co., 12 Gray, 265 ; Workman vs. Ins. Co., 2 La., 507.

This fact should particularly be borne in mind where the insurance is on goods or merchandise ; and if it be desired to restrict the risk, the specific portion of the building should be designated. . In all cases where the risk includes more than a main building it is better to add "and extension" or "wing," if such is the intention of the agent at the time. But such words should not be used to describe a detached adjacent structure, this is a separate building and should be so treated.

Peoria Co. vs. Ins. Co., 15 Ins. Law Jour., 52.

The term "dwelling" indicates that the principal use of the building is for purposes of private residence, and should never be used exclusively where it is in part used for other purposes, as for a store, a workshop, or for any purpose which increases the risk ; for the law is that if the term does not fairly indicate the real character of the premises or a part is occupied for purposes which by the provisions of the policy increase the risk the insurance will be forfeited, and the same rule applies to other classes of hazards.

White vs. Assurance Co., 8 Gray, 556; Sarsfield vs. Ins. Co., 61 Barb., 479; Lappin vs. Ins. Co., 58 Barb., 325 ; Franklin Ins. Co. vs. Martin, 8 Ins. Law Jour., 134.

Again, the terms building, dwelling, etc., include only such materials as are actually incorporated in them, not unfinished materials that may be on the ground and intended to be incorporated. .

Ellmaker vs. Ins. Co., 5 Penn. St., 183.

Store, mill, factory, etc., refer, as has been said, to the specific use of the property, and unless properly qualified, may include adjacent premises not intended to be covered, and will include not simply the buildings themselves, but such adjuncts in the shape of fixed machinery and the like as are essential to make a complete factory or mill. Where machinery or adjuncts of any kind, which are not strictly a part of the building, are to be included in a policy on the building, they should be separately mentioned, or specifically excluded if so intended.

Hews vs. Ins. Co., 8 Ins. Law Jour., 291; Harris vs. Ins. Co., 4 Ins. Law Jour., 799; Claffey vs. Ins. Co., 15 Ins. Law Jour., 237 ; Fair vs. Ins. Co., 4 Ins. Law Jour., 114 ; Liebenstein vs. Ins. Co., 45 Ill., 303.

The term "machinery" is a broad one, and has been sometimes extended by the courts to include tools and other appurtenances needed for a complete manufactory, as well as what is more strictly implied by the word, where such appeared to be the intention of the parties. In other cases it has been given a more restricted meaning, and tools have been distinguished as simple instruments used by hand. So implements used in connection with machinery have been held to constitute a part of it.

Lovewell vs. Ins. Co., 7 Ins. Law Jour., 672 ; Seavey vs. Ins. Co., 3 Ins. Law Jour., 576.

The term "tools" has also been given a very broad definition by the courts. In Lovewell vs. Ins. Cos., *supra*, the policy covered "their fixed and movable machinery, engines, lathes and tools," and it was held that the term "tools" included all patterns which from their size and shape admitted of being applied and managed by the hands of one man !

All such adjuncts of a manufacturing risk therefore should be separately specified whether excluded or otherwise, as "on fixed and movable machinery" (the one referring to that which attaches to the realty, the other to such as is of the nature of trade-fixtures) "except" or "including tools, patterns, engines, boilers," etc. But where these subjects are separately insured in the policy, this of itself will exclude them from the general class. The essential feature to be aimed at in describing a risk of any kind is to make the intention so clear that there can be no doubt what property is meant. The location of the property, by street and number if possible, is of course always essential, and in case of adjoining or adjacent structures on the same premises, all the distinctive marks needed to discriminate the particular building from the others, such as height, area, material, or use, should be added.

The temptation to describe a risk under some kindred name which will make it appear more favorable to the company is sometimes a strong one ; but is decidedly dangerous for the applicant. If the misrepresentation is material, or the apparent motive a fraudulent one, the insurance will be defeated. A saloon is not a hotel, and such a misdescription of a low rum-hole in Baker vs. Ins. Co. (15 Ins. Law Jour., 887) defeated the policy. In Loehner vs. Ins. Co. (19 Mo., 628) a house of ill fame was described as a dwelling, and the court ruled that if its use enhanced the risk the company was not liable. In Claffey vs. Ins. Co. (15 Ins. Law Jour., 237) property was insured as the "Wolf houses," and the claim was made that this description included a barn as part of the group. A town insurance company in Wisconsin was allowed to insure certain classes of risks only upon a vote of its members, one of such risks was a schoolhouse which had been insured as a dwelling, but had been altered for this purpose. The supreme court of that State declared in Luthe vs. Ins. Co. (12 Ins. Law Jour., 30) that the insurance was void. In Maher vs. Ins. Co. (6 Ins. Law Jour., 103) property which was in part used for a grocery was described by the agent as a dwelling, and so insured because he deemed the description sufficient. The doubts of the applicant regarding its property were actually quieted by the assurances of the agent; but the court refused to consider these facts and declared the contract forfeited.

These are a few of the many cases which might be cited, showing the importance of correctly designating the character of the risk.

PERSONAL PROPERTY.

Personal property as a subject of insurance differs in several important respects from buildings. The latter are fixed in one place, the former is movable. Hence, the designation of the location of personal property is generally the most important feature of the whole risk. Where insurance is on specific property of this kind the policy will follow the property from place to place unless the intention to insure only while in the place named clearly appears. Mere statements as to present location, such as "stored in barn," have sometimes been held to be intended only to designate more clearly the property covered and not to restrict its removal.

Everett vs. Ins. Co., 4 Ins. Law Jour., 121 ; Smith vs. Ins. Co., 32 N. Y., 399; Blood vs. Ins. Co., 12 Cush., 472.

The intention therefore to limit the policy to the place of storage or deposit should be made plain. The words ordinarily used for this purpose are "contained in." The courts are now agreed that these words will thus restrict the policy in the case of such subjects as furniture on storage or a stock-in-trade which could not reasonably be expected to be temporarily elsewhere as an incident to its use. But with regard to that large class of subjects whose use involves a frequent or even occasional removal, the clause will only mean that they are to be in the place designated when such use does not require their absence. Thus horses and wagons "contained in " a barn may be covered while in use on the road, or temporarily located elsewhere for repairs or in the prosecution of business. Wearing apparel may be covered while being worn on the street.

McCluer vs. Ins. Co., 5 Ins. Law Jour., 743 ; Noyes vs. Ins. Co., 15 Ins. Law Jour., 57, and cases there cited ; Phœnix Ins. Co. vs. Voorhis, 15 Ins. Law Jour., 865.

Special care on this point should be taken in case of such shifting risks as rolling-stock on steam and horse railroads which are likely to be absent the greater part of the time, and the provision should be added that "this policy applies only while contained in," etc., in all such cases. Unless the particular part of the building in which it is contained is also specified, the insured property can be removed to any other part. Thus a manufacturer insured while occupying only a single story, may afterwards extend his business to the whole building and be covered by a policy simply on stock contained in the building, or the occupant of one of three stores in one building may in the same way afterwards occupy them all by tearing away the partitions and converting them into a single store.

Fair vs. Ins. Co., 4 Ins. Law Jour., 114 ; West vs. Ins. Co., 9 Allen, 316.

A second feature in which personal property differs from buildings is that the latter are specific in their character, the former often is not. A policy on a building may cover slight alterations and additions so long as it remains substantially the same structure, but will not cover a new building put in the place of the old, or a building so altered as to be a substantially different structure.

Maryland Ins. Co. vs. Gusdorf, 5 Ins. Law Jour., 384 ; Fair vs. Ins. Co., 4 Ins. Law Jour., 114 ; Lyman vs. Ins. Co., 14 Allen, 329 ; Imbrey vs. Ins. Co., 5 Gray, 541.

But in the case of personal property the policy generally covers whatever property may be within the description at the time of loss, whether it be the specific material included at the time of contracting or not. An insurance on a stock of groceries or dry-goods allows the insured to sell and substitute other and different articles or to enlarge his stock. The articles composing household goods may be exchanged for others ; the only limitation being that the subject shall tally with the description. Hence it is important that any limitations which it is desired to impose on the substitution or addition of other articles should be clearly indicated in the policy. A policy on "the specific goods or furniture now contained in," etc., or "consisting of," etc., would not allow others to be added or substituted. An insurance on the "stock of groceries, excepting gasoline, gunpowder," etc., may be necessary to prevent such dangerous articles from being added to the stock; for the written portion of a policy will control provisions that are merely printed, and it has been frequently held that an insurance on a class of goods among which certain articles are generally kept, will be understood as a license to keep such articles, notwithstanding a printed provision to the contrary.

Amer. Ins. Co. vs. Rothschild, 82 Ill., 116 ; Germania Ins. Co. vs. Francis, 6 Ins. Law Jour., 235 ; Boynton vs. Ins. Co., 16 Barb., 254 ; Moadinger vs. Ins. Co., 2 Hall, 490.

The particular class of articles intended to be covered should be as strictly defined as their nature will admit. Such words as "contents" will include almost anything in the shape of personal property ; and, if employed, should be further qualified by "consisting of," etc., which limits the insurance to such as are enumerated, while the word "including" imposes no restrictions whatever, but rather the reverse.

Moadinger vs. Ins. Co., *supra;* Rafael vs. Ins. Co., 7 La. An., 244.

The terms "household goods" and "furniture" refer to those articles intended for the adornment or comfort of the house, which are removable at will. They do not include clothing and jewelry ; articles for consumption, such as food and coal ; nor goods that may be kept simply as merchandise for sale, unless such appears to have been the intention. "Clothing" and "wearing apparel" in like manner do not include jewelry.

Longueville vs. Ins. Co., 8 Ins. Law Jour., 845 ; Holmes vs. Ins. Co., 10 Met., 211 ; Clarey vs. Ins. Co., 1 Ben., 432.

Stock of "goods" and "merchandise," on the contrary, refer to chattels of any kind kept for sale ; while "stock-in-trade" may include even implements used in case of a manufacturing business. Like "contents," they are very broad, and should be further qualified when used.

Planters' Ins. Co. vs. Engle, 9 Ins. Law Jour., 71 ; Moadinger vs. Ins. Co., *supra;* Boynton vs. Ins. Co., 16 Barb., 254.

When properly qualified as "stock of hardware," or "dry-goods," or "groceries," only such articles will be included as belong to the particular class named. But if it is customary to include among such stock articles which are not strictly dry-goods or groceries, the courts will hold that the parties intended to cover them also in the policy. Thus, insurance on "his stock as a country grocer," will cover all those articles which it is usual for country grocers to keep.

Collins vs. Ins. Co., 8 Ins. Law Jour., 353 ; Medina vs. Ins. Co., 120 Mass., 225 ; Franklin Ins. Co. vs. Updegraff, 43 Penn. St., 353.

It frequently happens, too, that the class of goods thus insured includes articles which are expressly forbidden by the policy to be kept, or which are required to be specifically mentioned in order to be included. Now, the prevailing disposition of the courts is to overrule all such printed limitations and prohibitions, if the language used in describing the risk indicates an intention on the part of the agent to waive the prohibition. Thus, a policy as above on stock such as is "usually kept in a country store" has been allowed to override a prohibitory clause, the courts arguing that it was the intention to insure such prohibited articles as belong to the stock. Therefore, the intention on this point should be made plain in the description. "Except such as are herein prohibited," or, if the risks are classified in policy-schedules as "hazardous," etc., on "merchandise not hazardous," or language of similar import, will show that the parties intended to exclude the prohibited risks.

Jones vs. Ins. Co., 2 Ins. Law Jour., 186; Pindar vs. Ins. Co., 1 Ins. Law Jour., 127; Franklin Ins. Co. vs. Updegraff, *supra ;* Steinbach vs. Ins. Co., 8 Ins. Law Jour., 621.

It rarely happens that the subjects of insurance can be enumerated under one specific name, as pianos or wheat or horses; though this should be done, if possible, but the name must generally be that of a class, as hardware or wooden ware, etc. The rule, therefore, should be to describe the risk under that class name which is the most restricted as well as most expressive. Horned cattle should be insured as such, not simply as cattle or as live-stock, which latter will include poultry, hogs, horses, etc. Hardware should be insured as such, not simply as merchandise; and where articles prohibited in the policy are included in the stock, the intention either to exclude or include them should be made plain in the description. The effect of these various policy prohibitions will be considered more at length further on. All live-stock should be specially insured under its class name, as horses, oxen, etc.; not as contents, merchandise, and the like, for the latter are usually treated as referring simply to inanimate objects. Such vague words as contents and appliances should never be relied on as descriptive of property. In Washington Ins. Co. vs. Davison (30 Md., 91) the intention of the term apparatus in a factory risk extended the policy to virtually everything connected with the manufacture.

Not only is it to the interest of the company but also of the insured, that the subject-matter should be described as specifically as possible. Otherwise, property that was intended by the applicant to be included may not be covered. In Raphael vs. Ins. Co. (7 La. An., 244) the subject-matter was insured simply as "stock of jewelry and clothing," while it consisted also of musical and surgical instruments, guns, and books, all of which were thus excluded from the policy. In Burgess vs. Ins. Co. (10 Allen, 221) the insurance was on "merchandise" in certain buildings, and articles intended partly for use were excluded. A policy on a "stock of hair wrought, raw, and in process as a retail store," did not include such articles as were not hair. This neglect to indicate the specific character of the stock has led to repeated disputes in the courts. Stock in case of a manufacturer of any kind may mean much more than in case of a merchant. With the latter it is usually confined to goods for sale, with the former it may include all the articles used in carrying on his business. Thus in case of a furniture dealer it has included his varnish and oils, and in the case of a baker, his sieves, pans, and troughs.

Medina vs. Ins. Co., 120 Mass., 225 ; Moadinger vs. Ins. Co., 2 Hall, 490 ; Haley vs. Ins. Co., 12 Gray, 545.

So where the risk has simply been designated as a "starch factory" all the machinery, tools, and fixtures needed for the factory have been held to be included, and such terms as lumber-yard and ship-yard have sometimes been allowed to cover materials stored on the street, outside of the yard proper. A policy on a "saw-mill" was in like manner held to include the machinery ; hence, the importance of insuring mills, factories, churches, and the like as buildings.

Bigler vs. Ins. Co., 20 Barb., 635 ; Peoria Ins. Co. vs. Lewis, 18 Ill., 553 ; Webb vs. Ins. Co., 2 Sandf., 447.

Just what should be included in "machinery," too, has been repeatedly questioned, and since it has sometimes been extended to all those articles used in connection with the machinery proper, it should be further qualified when necessary. Engines and boiler-houses should be separated in the policy from factory buildings and machinery.

Leavey vs. Ins. Co., 111 Mass., 540 ; See also ante.

Every class of articles which can be appropriately separated from the rest should not only be specifically mentioned, but where practicable specifically insured, and in case of a subsequent increase of the amount insured under a renewal, the specific insurances should be re-apportioned in the renewal receipt, otherwise the renewal will be a general insurance of the whole.

Driggs vs. Ins. Co., 10 Barb., 440.

MEMORANDUM ARTICLES.

Where large values are concentrated in small compass, as in the case of money and jewelry, or where the articles are exceedingly fragile, as with plate-glass and decoration, or the subjects have a high value to the owner, but are comparatively worthless to others, as deeds and account-books, it is plain that without proper precautions a company may unwittingly be involved in a heavy loss or be called on to respond for an excessive claim. In regard to another large class like trade-fixtures, as has been seen, its status is often indefinite and liable to dispute. For these reasons all policies contain a list of memorandum articles which will not be covered unless specially mentioned. Articles thus specified will not be included under any term which may be merely descriptive of their general character. They will not form a part of insured "contents," watches will not be included in "wearing apparel," manuscripts will not be covered by a policy on "books," nor plate-glass windows by insurance on the "building," where these are among the memorandum articles. Where insurance is desired the subject must be mentioned under its particular name, as watch, or jewelry, or plate-glass.

The uncertain value of many memorandum articles furnishes a strong objection against their insurance at all by the companies, and when property of this character is insured, whether strictly speaking a memorandum article or not, care should be exercised about its valuation. For insurance purposes the value of an article is only what it would bring if sold, not what it may be worth to the owner; that is its legal value. A manuscript may represent years of work, a deed or account-book if lost would perhaps secure a handsome reward for its return, but none of them would have any commercial value and are practically uninsurable. All subjects having a very uncertain commercial value, such as pictures and statuary, should be insured with great caution, and if covered at all, shculd be by schedule naming a separate valuation on each.

SPECIFIC DESCRIPTION OF THE PROPERTY.

Not only is it important that the character of the risk as a dwelling, planing-mill, stock of hardware, etc., be correctly stated, but that all details that may be inquired about (and such as are not inquired about, if they essentially modify the character of the risk) should also be fully and correctly given. In Steinmetz vs. Ins. Co. (6 Phila., 21) the use of a fifth story by nine or ten persons regularly employed in making shades, converted the building in part into a factory, and the failure to state the fact forfeited the policy. In Mathews vs. Ins. Co. (2 Cin. Sup. Ct., 109) the policy was on a "planing-mill and saw-mill;" one story, however, was used as a carpenter's shop, and the failure to state this fact forfeited the policy. In Dewees vs. Ins. Co. (35 N. J., 366) property was insured as a "country store," but it turned out that a part of it was being used as a stable, and the insurance was avoided. In Lapin vs. Ins. Co.

(58 Barb., 325) property insured as a "dwelling" was used in part as a saloon, and the policy was forfeited.

These cases illustrate the importance of furnishing full details regarding such matters as may modify the character of the risk, even though there may be nothing in the application or policy directing special attention to them. So in regard to personal property, as has been already pointed out, property insured under any class name as hardware, drygoods, cattle, and the like will only cover such as the parties evidently intended by the term used. Thus, in Allegre vs. Ins. Co. (8 G. & J., 190), the court declared that an insurance on live-stock must be specific, they could not be covered simply by a policy on the cargo; and in Wolcott vs. Ins. Co. (4 Pick., 449), neither the animals nor their food were allowed to be included in such a policy, while, as will be shown farther on, the presence of prohibited articles or employments may forfeit the entire policy. In Appleby vs. Ins. Co. (54 N. Y., 253) a policy covering cabinet ware, which is a finished article, was avoided by the added work of putting together and finishing chairs as well.

When inquiry is made as to the height of the building, the cellar is not in law one of the stories; neither, perhaps, would an attic be included in case of a peaked roof, but if there be a basement it should be mentioned; and the same is true of an attic if substantially a story.

Benedict vs. Ins. Co., 1 Daly, 8.

The dimensions of a building materially affect the risk, whether it be height or ground area, and whether in respect to the main building or to wings; concealment and misrepresentation regarding these matters has been treated as just ground for forfeiture by the courts. In Casey vs. Goldsmid (2 L. C. R., 200) the presence of an adjoining building in the nature of an extension which was not disclosed was deemed, if fraudulent, sufficient to forfeit the insurance. In Chase vs. Ins. Co. (20 N. Y., 52) the failure to disclose a kitchen attached to the main building forfeited the policy; while in Perry Ins. Co. vs. Stewart (19 Penn. St., 45) the conformity of such a kitchen to the description was the subject of litigation. In Pim vs. Reed (6 M. & G., 1) a building was described as two-story, and the subsequent addition of a third story was declared to be an increase of risk which worked a forfeiture.

In like manner the materials of which the building is composed, the nature of the roof, partitions, parapet walls, and all the more important features of the construction are even more material than mere size, and misrepresentations regarding them have been repeated grounds of forfeiture. In Chase vs. Ins. Co., *supra*, the building was described as a "stone dwelling-house," while the attached kitchen was wood, and the

court held that the proposition was to insure a stone house, there was
no contract regarding a building partly of wood. In Day vs. Ins. Co.
(52 Me., 60) a mill was described as of certain dimensions, and declared
to be separated from other buildings, whereas it had an extension beyond
the main building, and this defeated the policy. In Gerhauser vs. Ins.
Co. (7 Nevada, 174) a "brick building" proved to have wood temporarily substituted in one of the walls, which resulted in litigation. So in
Woods vs. Ins. Co. (50 Mo., 112) a building partly of wood was described as brick, and the question for the jury was whether the fault lay
with the insured or the agent.

Defective Descriptions in Policy Writing Illustrated.

The great importance of accurately and correctly describing the insured subject justifies its special emphasis. After what has just been
said there is, perhaps, no better way of illustrating what is, and what is
not, an adequate description than by citing a few of the cases which have
come before the courts.

In Mason vs. Ins. Co. (12 G. & J., 468) the policy was on a "bark
now being built." It did not cover materials lying in the ship-yard ready
to be put in, these were not a component part of the bark, and should
have been specified if insurance was desired. In New York Gas Light
Co. vs. Ins. Co. the policies were on gasometers and fixtures to be
placed in buildings of the insured's subscribers. The stock of gasometers
and fixtures, which at the time of insuring only amounted to $7,000, was
afterwards increased to $120,000. The failure to limit the amount at
the time of insuring allowed the hazard to be increased to seventeen
times the original amount, and converted it into a huge blanket risk. In
Moadinger vs. Ins. Co. (2 Hall, 490) an insurance simply on "his stock-
in-trade as a baker," allowed recovery not only for all the tools and implements, but for a horse and cart used in the business. It should have
been further described as "consisting of." In Crosby vs. Ins. Co. (5
Gray, 504) the policy was "on their stock of watches, watch trimmings,
etc.," and was found to cover the entire stock of plate, silver ware, and
even tools. The "etc." proved an omnibus addition to the risk. In
White vs. Ins. Co. (8 Gray, 566) the policy was on a dwelling and "wood-
house." The wood-house proved to be a joint wood-house and carriage-
house, all under one roof. In Burr vs. Ins. Co. (16 N. Y., 267) the
policy was on a "three and a half story, brick building, slate roof, coped,
occupied as a cordage factory, situated northwest corner of," etc. The
insured owned two buildings nearly alike, one on the southwest, the other
on the northwest corner, but it was the former that was used as a cordage

factory, the latter was a block factory; hence, a dispute as to which was covered when the fire came. In Liddle vs. Ins. Co. (43 Bosw., 179) the insurance was on goods in a "corner store," and the policy was indorsed : "The communication in the adjoining stores does not prejudice this insurance." The insured was occupying both of the communicating stores. A statement of the ground area of the corner store would have obviated dispute.

In Lycoming Ins. Co. vs. Updegraff (46 Pa., 311) the insurance was on goods in "new frame" wareroom, to which a brick extension was afterwards added, but the qualification as to "frame" saved the company from a loss in the extension. In Peoria Ins. Co. vs. Hall (12 Mich., 202) the insurance by a partner, in his individual name, without any special intention of benefiting the firm, prevented him from recovering more than his own interest in the property. In Burgess vs. Ins. Co. (10 Allen, 221) the court made this important distinction : A policy on "merchandise," contained, etc., will not cover articles kept partly for use, but a policy on "property" will include both those for sale and for use. In Liebenstein vs. Ins. Co. (45 Ill., 301) two policies were written, one on stock in a "chair factory," the other on stock in a "two-story, frame building occupied as a chair factory." In the first the insurance was extended to the stock in a second building, which was used in connection with the main factory ; while in the other it was limited to the single building intended by the company. In N. A. Ins. Co. vs. Throop (22 Mich., 146) the insurance was on stock, lumber, and goods "in said building." The addition of the latter clause saved the company from a loss on lumber lying outside the building. In Hewitt vs. Ins. Co. (10 Ins. Law Jour., 375) the insurance was "on grain in stacks," and was allowed to include a quantity of flax which had been stacked and was unthreshed, though the court admitted that it was doubtful whether flax would in all cases be considered grain. The failure to exclude a doubtful item resulted in its inclusion. The term grain should be applied only to those products popularly known as such ; while all others, such as flax, hay, and the like should be excepted, if necessary, to avoid dispute. Joel vs. Harvey, (5 W. R., 488) illustrates this : The policy was on "stock-in-trade, consisting of corn, seed, hay, straw, fixtures, and utensils," and hops and matting were excluded, though a part of the stock.

In Pitney vs. Ins. Co. (4 Ins. Law Jour., 765) the policy insured P. only, whereas G. had a part interest ; to correct the mistake and cover the interest of the latter, the agent indorsed "loss payable one-half to G. as interest may appear." A more accurate statement setting forth that G. was part owner, and that the policy was changed to insure the interest of both ; or, better still, a cancellation and a new policy correctly written, might have saved a lawsuit. In Sawyer vs. Ins. Co. (37 Wis., 503) a part of the insurance was specified to be on property in section 19, but there was also insured "grain in stack" and "live-stock running at large." The failure to specifically restrict these also allowed the policy to cover grain and live-stock outside of the section. The words "held in trust" have frequently proved an omnibus clause to the disadvantage of the insurer. In Stillwell vs. Staples they covered stock intrusted for manufacture; in Rafel vs. Ins. Co. they covered goods in pawn. The case of Sherman vs. Ins. Co. (5 Ins. Law Jour., 285) illustrates the importance of specific insurance. Three companies insured on live-stock, among which was at least one very valuable animal. Three animals that were lost were worth only $113 apiece, but the fourth was worth $2,000. Two companies limited the amount of their liability on any one animal, the other did not. The liability of the latter was in consequence double that of the others. The case of Commonwealth vs. Ins. Co. (112 Mass., 136) conversely illustrates the most faulty kind of blanket insurance. The policy was on "all or either of their freight buildings," of which there were several, and it was held liable for its full amount on each, notwithstanding they were elsewhere specifically insured.

In Jackson vs. Ins. Co. (14 Ins. Law Jour., 546) the description of a building as "hard-finished," when this was true of only one story, caused the reinsurer to dispute its liability. In Eggleston vs. Ins. Co. (14 Ins. Law Jour., 365) the agent described the property as in a certain town, whereas it was in an addition adjoining the town, and the loss was disputed. In Mullville vs. Ins. Co. (13 Ins. Law Jour., 435) a diagram of the ground-plan of certain buildings, furnished by the insured in connection with the application, was treated by the agent as if a complete diagram of the property, and insurance was procured on a copy of it made by him. In point of fact, it failed to indicate intervening structures, which materially increased the risk, and the company was compelled to be responsible for the error.

LOCATION AND SURROUNDINGS OF THE RISK.

The specific location of a building or of contents should be defined as clearly as possible, both to avoid any doubt as to the subject-matter and to prevent removal. Frame buildings are sometimes moved, and the insurance would otherwise follow them unless the risk were increased.

Griswold vs. Ins. Co., 3 Ins. Law Jour., 254.

Personal property is essentially movable in its character. In Everett vs. Ins. Co. (4 Ins. Law Jour., 121) a threshing-machine was described as on a certain section and again as "stored in barn;" there was no such section, and it required a lawsuit to determine whether it was covered. In Bowman vs. Ins. Co. (5 Ins. Law Jour., 9) grain was described as in "barns" and in "Barn No. 2 north from house;" there was no barn north from the house, and again a suit was needed to determine the liability. In Sawyer vs. Ins. Co. (37 Wis., 503) insurance was on grain in stack. The insured afterwards purchased another farm and by reason of failure to limit the location the policy was held to cover on the new farm as well as the old. In Peterson vs. Ins. Co. (24 Iowa, 494) horses were insured with other property "situated" on a described farm, and it was held that the word was only descriptive, the horses were covered while absent on business. So in Noyes vs. Ins. Co. (15 Ins. Law Jour., 57) a sealskin dolman was insured as "contained in" a house, but was covered while absent for repairs; it was held that the words only meant that the house was the usual place of deposit. Both of these were cases where the property might be expected to be temporarily absent and should have been insured "only while contained in." In Broadwater vs. Ins. Co. (15 Ins. Law Jour., 295) the property was described as "their buildings adjoining and communicating—situated detached." They were not in fact detached from each other at all, but as they were detached from others, the company was held responsible for the faulty description by its agent. The buildings, too, while themselves belonging to the insured as a post-trader were on government land, but the fact that they were stated to be used by a post-trader was allowed to override a stipulation regarding the title. In Fair vs. Ins. Co. (4 Ins. Law Jour., 114) goods were insured as "contained in the Hunt building, situate on Main Street as per plan filed." The plan exhibited a building divided into three stores. The particular store occupied by the insured was not designated, and he was consequently able, by knocking down the partitions, to cover goods in all three. In Blake vs. Ins. Co. (12 Gray, 265) the property was described as in a building known as the car factory. A hole less than three feet square opened into an adjoining building which was used in connection with the factory, and was therefore held to be a wing. The failure to limit the description to the main building extended the policy to the wing.

These are a few of the numerous illustrations which can be cited of the consequences of imperfect and faulty descriptions of location, and of the importance of such a description as shall not be open to dispute.

EXPOSURES.

Adjacent buildings when inquired about, should be fully described, and their distances noted. The proximity of such buildings is universally recognized as increasing the danger from fire, and is regarded by the courts as a material matter in which concealment will vitiate the insurance. All permanent structures within the specified distance should be mentioned and their correct distance and direction given, no matter whether they are large or small or their uses are important or otherwise. A failure to observe this rule has repeatedly caused a forfeiture of the policy. The distance should be that between the nearest parts. The same holds true regarding a diagram, it must be an accurate as well as complete map of the surroundings.

Burrett vs. Ins. Co., 5 Hill, 188 ; Wright vs. Ins. Co., 4 Ins. Law Jour., 251 ; O'Neil vs. Ins. Co., Hine & Nichols' Dig., 82 ; Chaffee vs. Co., 18 N. Y., 376; Continental Ins. Co. vs. Ware, 9 Ins. Law Jour., 519.

The subsequent erection of adjacent buildings by other parties is a matter on which the insurer should be informed, and if such information is called for by the policy its neglect may be fatal. Where such buildings are erected by the insured or within his control, the company should always be notified whether required by the policy or not ; for, if the risk is thereby materially increased, the insurance may be forfeited.

Pottsville Ins. Co. vs. Horan, 9 Ins. Law Jour., 201 ; Howard vs. Ins. Co., 13 B. Mon., 289 ; Stebbins vs. Ins. Co., 2 Hall, 632 ; Calvert vs. Ins. Co., 1 Allen, 308.

The same doctrine applies to any essential modifications in the character or use of adjacent premises which are likely to increase the risk, a matter which will be considered more at length further on.

Internal Appurtenances and Arrangements of Buildings.

In all special hazards great stress is laid by underwriters on such interior features and appurtenances as methods of heating and lighting, steam power, character and location of machinery, force-pumps, water-supply, watchmen, etc. Careful inquiries are usually made on these and other like points, and representations made by the insured regarding them are treated as warranties. The statements made, therefore, should be substantially correct. If any of the inquiries pertain to matters which are supposed to be of a permanent character the courts regard such inquiries as continuing warranties, that is, that the conditions represented to exist shall continue during the life of the policy. In that case any breach of the representation, even if made after the insurance had been effected, would result in forfeiture. Especially is this true of changes which are likely to increase the risk. Sometimes, too, the application provides that such representations shall continue to be true.

Aurora Ins. Co. vs. Eddy, 50 Ill., 106 ; Ripley vs. Ins. Co., 30 N. Y., 136; Farmers' Ins. Co. vs. Snyder, 16 Wend., 481 ; Dale vs. Ins. Co., 15 W. C., 175.

The applicant in case of a special hazard should understand that in regard to nearly all representations of this character, they are looked on by the companies as expressing not simply the existing condition of the risk, but that which will continue during the life of the policy. As the courts have well said, they are the inducements for taking the risk, and payment has frequently been forfeited because the actual status at the time of loss was different from that represented. The introduction of steam power into a mill previously run by water; the character of the machinery; the method of connecting the heating apparatus ; the nature of that apparatus or its presence at all ; the method and time of lighting,—all have reference to the existence of fire or of conditions likely to incite combustion within the building. They go far to determine the character of the risk, and are properly regarded as material matters by the courts.

In Daniels vs. Ins. Co. (10 Ins. Law Jour., 658) fires or lights were prohibited in a business where naphtha was employed, and the court declared that the use of a small stove for heating the naphtha was an increase of risk which forfeited the insurance. In Murdock vs. Ins. Co. (2 N. Y., 210) the applicant represented that a chimney would be built for the stovepipe, which passed through a window. Instead of doing so, the stove was moved and the pipe passed through a stone placed on the roof, and the policy was avoided. In Glen vs. Lewis (8 W. H. & G., 607) the temporary introduction of a steam-engine merely for trial in the face of a policy prohibition avoided the insurance, and in Robinson vs. Ins. Co. (3 Dutch, 134) the policy was defeated by subsequently locating a steam-engine in a building adjoining, which increased the risk, though no express prohibition was involved. Again, in Diehl vs. Ins. Co. (58 Pa. St., 443), the insurance was on a "tannery without steam" in which this was one of the clauses in the policy, and it was defeated by the subsequent addition of steam, regardless of any increase of risk. In Atkins vs. Ins. Co. (8 Ins. Law Jour., 78) the risk was a saw-mill, but the failure of the applicant to state the presence of a planing-machine forfeited the policy. So in 53 Texas, 61, the presence of a cotton-gin in a factory was adjudged fatal.

FORCE-PUMPS, WATER-SUPPLY, AND WATCHMEN.

Of equal importance with those last referred to are such inquiries as relate to the means of extinguishing and preventing fires. Representations regarding the presence of watchmen, fo ce-pumps, stand-pipes, tanks, and the like are looked on by the companies and generally by the courts as continuing warranties. Payments have been refused because the representions made regarding them have been found to be untrue at the time of loss. Inquiries about them should not be limited to their existence, but should extend to their efficiency. The company expects that a pump will be kept in order, that tanks will be filled, and that watchmen will not consist simply of periodical visitors, but of men on duty on the premises at the proper hours. Failure in these respects has involved litigations. Not only the application but frequently the policy contains stipulations regarding these precautionary measures, with which the insured is bound to comply. A policy on a quartz-mill provided that a watchman should be employed to guard the premises when idle. The so-called watchman proved to be a miner who was working nearly half a mile away during the day, and slept in a house nine hundred feet distant at night! The court held in Wenzel vs. Ins. Co. (14 Ins. Law Jour., 809) that this was not a compliance. Trojan Company vs. Ins. Co. (14 Ins. Law Jour., 625) was a similar case. The stipulation was that the watchman should be upon the premises night and day. In point of fact he slept in a house a hundred feet distant, and kept a representative in the shape of a watch-dog in the building. The court held that this was no compliance. So in Blumer vs. Ins. Co. (7 Ins. Law Jour., 833, and 9 Ins. Law Jour., 444) the court declared in both cases that a representation that one or two hands slept in the mill was a continuing warranty, and their absence forfeited the policy. In Miller vs. Ins. Co. (6 Ins. Law Jour., 873) the insured, in response to a question whether it was in charge of some person on the premises, replied, ''There is a man on the premises ;'' this was adjudged a continuing warranty. The case of Albion Lead Works vs. Ins. Co. (9 Ins. Law Jour., 435) is instructive. Instead of a written application, insurance was made on a mill property on an old description which included a watchman and the oral representation of a broker that there was a force-pump in working order. There was no watchman, and the pump was out of order. The court held that if they had been written representations of an existing condition they would have been continuing warranties. Because they were not the company had to pay the loss. In Sayles vs. Ins. Co. (2 Curt., 612) a warranty regarding force-pumps ready for use was held to include a warranty of power to work them, and in Gloucester Co. vs. Ins. Co. (5 Gray, 497) a similar representation regarding water-tanks was held to imply that they should be well filled from the time the building, which was unfinished, was completed.

The conclusion from these cases is that statements regarding these various appurtenances of building risks should embody no essentially false or evasive representations ; they should show not simply what is the subsisting, but what will be the continuing condition of the risk.

Use or Occupation of the Premises.

Closely allied with those features of the risk just referred to, is the use to which the insured premises may be put. A building is insured as a dwelling, or store, or factory in the expectation that it will continue to be used for that purpose. The use to which the premises are put is, as we have seen, a material feature in the description of the property, and a designation which is misleading, such as describing a building used in part for a stable as a dwelling, or a saloon as a hotel, will frequently forfeit the insurance. This is equally true whether the policy is on the building itself or the contents. A subsequent change in the use of a building will not always have this effect; but if it is forbidden by the policy, or materially increases the risk, or so radically alters its character that it becomes substantially an altogether different subject of insurance, the policy will no longer apply.

Fire Ass'n vs. Williamson, 26 Penn. St., 196 ; Hobby vs. Dana, 17 Barb., 111 ; Howell vs. Balt. Soc., 16 Md., 377 ; Appleby vs. Ins. Co., 45 Barb., 454.

Since nearly all policies contain provisions against increase of risk, and frequently prohibit explicitly the existence of certain classes of hazards, any material change in the occupation of the property, whether in whole or in part, may be dangerous to the insured, and the company should be informed. Where there is reason to apprehend that such a change may be made the policy should be written "only to be used as," etc. ; for, unless there is a distinct prohibition or a manifest increase in the risk, the courts are disposed to grant to the insured the largest license in the use of the premises consistent with the contract, and it is difficult for the company in many instances to satisfy a jury that the risk has been altered to its detriment. Thus in Richards vs. Ins. Co. (15 Ins. Law Jour., 598) premises improperly described as used for residence and stores were in part used for a restaurant and bakery, to which a brick oven was also attached. These facts, from an insurance standpoint, essentially altered the character of the risk, but they were regarded by the court in this instance rather as minor features in an imperfect general description, for which the agent was at fault. In contrast with this case, however, may be cited that of Fire Association vs. Williamson, *ante*, where three adjoining buildings were insured under one policy, one of which was at the time occupied as a shoe store ; but it was afterwards, without the knowledge of the company, changed to a grocery. The policy required grocery stores to be specified, and a higher rate was charged for them. The court ruled that the change of occupation vitiated the insurance as to all of the buildings.

Particularly in the case of special hazards are minute inquiries addressed to the insured in the application, not simply as to the general occupancy of the premises, but in regard to such details as the presence of planers, the disposition of shavings, the use of paints and varnishes; in case of saw-mills, whether custom or lumber work is done; whether it is also a lath and shingle mill; in case of breweries, regarding malt-kilns and stills; or in case of pork-houses, regarding slaughtering, rendering, and cutting; and so of other classes of risks. All such detailed inquiries are material in their character and must be truly answered; and where, as is often the case, the insured covenants against a subsequent increase of risk, any serious change subsequently introduced may jeopardize his policy. Thus, in People's Ins. Co. vs. Spencer (53 Penn. St., 353) the subject of insurance was a brewery, to which the work of distilling was subsequently added, and it was held to be a fatal increase of risk. So in Hervey vs. Ins. Co. (11 U. C. C. P., 394) a printing-office was subsequently added to a store risk without notifying the company, and the insurance was defeated. In Mayor vs. Ins. Co. (9 Bosw., 424) the court declared, that if buildings erected for exhibition purposes, and insured as such, were afterwards used for other purposes, it would be fatal. In Washington Co. Ins. Co. vs. Ins. Co. (5 Ohio St., 450) the court declared that the underwriter insuring a mechanical establishment is presumed to insure only against risks arising from the usual and appropriate mode of carrying on such business; the introduction of a new and unusual invention without the company's consent may, by increasing the risk, avoid the policy. In Cole vs. Ins. Co. (14 Ins. Law Jour., 453) the court declared that the addition of a drying-house in close proximity to a planing-mill was a self-evident increase of risk, which barred recovery. In German-American Ins. Co. vs. Steiger (13 Ins. Law Jour., 487) it was held that the substitution of a fire for a steam drier presented a question for the jury whether the risk had thereby been increased. In nearly all cases of special hazards the survey is made part of the policy, and the universal rule of the courts in that case is that those matters regarding which questions are asked are thereby made warranties, and a substantial breach will forfeit the insurance.

Le Roy vs. Ins. Co., 39 N. Y., 90 ; Cox vs. Ins. Co., 29 Ind., 586 ; Le Roy vs. Ins. Co., 6 Hand., 80.

The agent should see to it, not only that the answers are correctly given by the insured, but that all the questions are answered as far as possible, for the omission of answers may leave the insured at liberty to alter the character of the risk in those respects to any extent which is not an obvious increase of hazard.

Lorillard Ins. Co. vs. McCulloch, 21 O. St., 176.

Specific Titles or Interests.

OWNERSHIP.

The principal interest in property, and that which should be insured in preference to any other, is ownership, by which the companies usually understand the strictly legal title, with the right to control and dispose of the property. This interest is generally designated in the application and policy by the word "his" or "owner." These words, however, should never be used without proper qualification, unless the insured has the legal title and right of disposal for his own benefit. For in law they are frequently allowed to support any loose claim where the insured might regard himself as the owner in a popular sense, and where his interest is much less than that of an actual title in fee. Thus, a man has been allowed to designate as "his," buildings on leased ground or belonging to his wife, and to call himself the "owner" of property which he had only contracted to purchase, or to which his title was at best but an equitable one. In repeated instances the companies have thus been led to believe that they were insuring an absolute and unqualified ownership, whereas events proved that the interest was qualified in its character.

Hough vs. Ins. Co., 29 Conn., 10; Pierce vs. Ins. Co., 62 Barb., 636.

To guard against this, the policy usually stipulates that the precise nature of the title, if qualified, shall be stated ; and then a failure to do so, unless the agent is in fault, will vitiate the insurance.

Porter vs. Ins. Co., 6 Ins. Law Jour., 928 ; Ætna Ins. Co. vs. Resh, 8 Ins. Law Jour., 271 ; Murphry vs. Ins. Co., 5 Ins. Law Jour., 297.

The ordinary provision is that if the interest be other than the "entire and unconditional ownership" or "absolute and sole ownership for the use and benefit of the insured," it must be so stated. To meet such requirements, the estate should be vested in fee-simple, with an absolute power of disposal, not simply for a term of years, or for life, or under certain circumstances; it should belong solely to the party and for his own benefit. If no title-deed has passed, there should be at least an undisputed right to compel it. There may be mortgages and liens upon the property, provided they are mere liens that do not affect the title or right of possession. But these should be separately noted, for here again the policy usually provides that failure in this respect will result in forfeiture.

It occasionally happens that while the insured is the unqualified owner of the building, his ownership of the land on which it stands is qualified or the title is in another. Where the language of the contract clearly includes both land and building, as it usually does, a failure to state the qualified interest will be fatal ; and in all cases such qualified interest in the land should be stated, both to avoid dispute and because buildings standing upon the land of another are actually less valuable to the owner. They are liable to removal at the expiration of a lease, and are a temptation to fraudulent insurance.

Washington Mills Co. vs. Ins. Co., 13 Ins. Law Jour., 225, and cases there cited.

In all other cases where the ownership is not of the absolute character described above, it should be treated as qualified and its precise nature stated. In no case should mortgages or mere incumbrances of any kind be treated as ownership. Ordinary tenancies do not conflict with the absolute ownership of the landlord, but life-tenancies and other freehold interests do conflict with the absolute title of the reversioner or remainder-man. . Possession and control by other parties than the insured should always be noted. In Wenzel vs. Ins. Co. (14 Ins. Law Jour., 809) the leasing and surrendering control to other parties was declared to be a change of possession within the meaning of the policy.

See Woody vs. Ins. Co., 9 Ins. Law Jour., 276 ; Cheek vs. Ins. Co., *supra ;* Davis vs. Ins. Co., 15 Ins. Law Jour., 533 ; Clay Ins. Co. vs. Mfg. Co., 4 Ins. Law Jour., 858 ; Porter vs. Ins. Co., 6 Ins. Law Jour., 928 ; Lycoming Ins. Co. vs. Haven, 7 Ins. Law Jour., 449.

Property belonging to the wife should be insured as hers, not as her husband's.

Hunt vs. Ins. Co., 14 Ins. Law Jour., 298 ; Agricultural Ins. Co. vs. Montague, 7 Ins. Law Jour., 708.

Part-owners should be allowed to insure only to the extent of their interest, unless authorized to insure for the remaining owners and in the name of all. Partners are thus authorized if their intention to do so clearly appears.

Peoria Ins. Co. vs. Hall, 12 Mich., 202.

As a matter of good practice, an agent should decline all risks where the ownership is doubtful, or mixed, or otherwise unsatisfactory. It is a great deal better to avoid possible difficulty than to go in carelessly and get out skillfully. The following points are given, however, so that the agent may understand the legal conditions of each class of cases and be intelligent in his declinations as well as in his acceptances.

In the case of buildings and real estate there is not often any question as to what will constitute a legal ownership. But with personal property it is different. Here the actual possession of the goods or chattels is likely to seriously affect the property rights, and the title to goods in the possession or control of one party which are claimed by another should be closely scrutinized. In many of the States it is an established rule that the legal title to personal property which has been mortgaged, especially if placed within the control of the mortgagee, vests in the latter.

Appleton Iron Co. vs. Ins. Co., 8 Ins. Law Jour., 177 ; Kronk vs. Ins. Co., 9 Ins. Law Jour., 26.

In case of ordinary sales of personal property where the purchaser has not yet come into possession, if it be a specific article, as a horse, the latter is the owner ; but if it be an undefined portion of a lot of goods, as a hundred bushels of corn from a granary, or if anything remains to be done to complete the sale, the title remains with the seller until the specific amount has been set aside and accepted by the purchaser, or the act omitted has been done.

Merchants' Bank vs. Bangs, 102 Mass., 295 ; Haley vs. Ins. Co., 120 Mass. 292 ; Suffolk Ins. Co. vs. Boyden, 9 Allen, 123.

In the same way, articles that have been ordered and are in process of construction remain the property of the maker until delivered or accepted ; and a building in process of erection under contract will remain at the risk of the builder until accepted by the owner.

Filden vs. Besley, 9 Ins. Law Jour., 241 ; Commercial Ins. Co. vs. Ins. Co., 16 Ins. Law Jour., 81.

The further fact that a party in possession of personal property under circumstances which will justify a belief in his ownership can wrongfully pass a title to innocent purchasers, again enhances the risk of insurance in such cases. What are known as fixtures often give rise to embarrassing questions of ownership, which will be considered hereafter. The questions of possession and control, therefore, become important matters for consideration in all insurances on personal property. Where the character of the interest cannot be satisfactorily determined, it is better to insure the owner of the property, briefly stating the facts, with loss payable to John Doe, the party wanting protection, "as interest shall appear."

To meet the delicate questions regarding ownership of goods which have been bargained for but still remain in the hands of the seller, two phrases are in common use among underwriters : "Sold but not removed," and "sold but not delivered." The first applies to goods the title to which has actually passed to the purchaser. The second applies to those where the title still remains with the seller, and is not really needed at all in most cases, since the policy already covers all goods while they remain his property. It is the policy of the companies to limit their protection as far as possible to the party or parties named in the contract, and to discourage the insertion of either clause when not actually required.

Waring vs. Ins. Co., 1 Ins. Law Jour., 672.

QUALIFIED AND LIMITED ESTATES.

Interests in property other than that of absolute and unqualified legal ownership should generally be insured simply as "his interest," stating its character ; or, if the applicant has no actual interest of his own which will authorize him to receive the money, but is simply acting as the representative or agent of those who would be entitled to receive it, the insurance should be directly on the interest of the latter or for their benefit.

Martin vs. Ins. Co., 15 Ins. Law Jour., 371.

Prominent among such interests are life-estates, including the dower rights of widows when limited to life, which are often erroneously described as ownerships, but which are in reality mere tenancies lasting during life. It is plain that the interest of such parties must generally be less than the actual value of the property, depending upon the age of the tenant, and is usually computed by multiplying the net rental value by the expectancy of life at the given age as shown by a mortality table, but this will give an exaggerated value unless the tenant be of advanced age. Life-tenants are often invested with the duty of caring for and keeping the property insured. But in such case they are acting for the reversioners as well as themselves, and the insurance should be for the benefit of themselves and the reversioners. Whoever has the charge of such property is the proper party to effect the insurance, which should be for the benefit of all rather than a particular interest when this can be done. Thus, if the property is that of an estate, it may be insured for the benefit of the estate ; or, what is better, for the benefit of the life-tenant and heirs or devisees.

Clinton vs. Ins. Co., 1 Ins. Law Jour., 436 ; Clinton vs. Ins. Co., 51 Barb., 647.

The great objection to all separate insurances of minor or partial interests is that different parties may thus independently insure the property for several times its value, and not only is a temptation furnished to fraud, but the question of adjustment becomes an embarrassing one for the companies. It is well, however, for the agent to understand that the companies have a short-cut to justice through the replacement or rebuilding clause, and when a case of multiplied overinsurances is up for discussion, and the question is asked, "What would the companies do in case of the burning of property so overinsured ?" the prompt and ready answer would be, "They would replace the property."

But, of course, there are many instances where such limited insurance is required, and the agent should be familiar with the rights of the parties. The interest of the reversioner, like that of the life-tenant, may be the subject of insurance, and the value of such an interest is the reverse of the other. It is the present worth of the sum which the building or other property, in view of its depreciation, would be valued at at the end of the probable life of the tenant. Unless the latter is an elderly person, such an interest is usually very small, and hardly a fit subject for separate insurance. This class of risks is to be avoided unless special authority is obtained from the company. So also in regard to all the partial interests and other complicated or intangible insurable interests herein treated. The mere fact that a man has a legal right to obtain insurance does not by any means constitute him a desirable customer.

Ordinary tenancies for a term of years and all leasehold interests create insurable interests ; but only where the tenant is liable to pay rent after a destruction by fire, or the rent is paid in advance, or where the actual value of the use through improvements made by himself is in excess of the rental, and his insurable interest is only such liability or excess. Except where buildings have been erected by the lessee, or he is bound to replace, this interest is of such a vague character that it should seldom be covered. In any case the specific character of the interest covered should be carefully defined, otherwise injuries which are merely consequential in their character are likely to be included.

Niblo vs. Ins. Co., 1 Sandf., 551 ; Mayor vs. Ins. Co., 10 Bos., 537 ; Cushman vs. Ins. Co., 34 Me., 487 ; Imp. F. Ins. Co. vs. Murray, 73 Penn. St., 13.

In the same way, rentals might be insured by landlords, and such intangible interests as expected incomes and profits, or consequential damages resulting from business injuries, or expenses on account of fire, are allowed by the law to be insured. But such risks are not included under ordinary policies on the property ; they must be specifically stated if insured at all, and it is a well-established principle in fire underwriting that the insurance of consequential injuries is in the highest degree unsatisfactory in its workings and results, and except in rare cases should be refused.

Niblo vs. Ins. Co., 1 Sandf., 551; Leonards vs. Ins. Co., 2 Rob., 131.

TRUSTEESHIPS.

Trustees of various kinds, who have been intrusted with tne control of property belonging to others, constitute a numerous class, who are recognized in law as having qualified titles or interests which they may insure. Such are warehousemen, commission merchants, executors and administrators, and, in short, all parties having the custody of such property. But the general doctrine is that, except in the case of common carriers, trustees are not liable for losses by fire unless by some stipulation or special responsibility imposed on them, or in cases of negligence, and insurance by them may be said to be voluntary.

Rice vs. Nixon, 14 Ins. Law Jour., 329.

This is the ordinary rule regarding goods consigned to the possession of others for various purposes. But there are cases, such as that of a trustee having the care of an estate, where insurance may be obligatory. This question of responsibility on the part of the trustee is an important one for the agent to consider. In some policies the responsibility in the case of goods held in trust has been expressly limited by the words "for which he is responsible," and in such case no others will be included. These or similar words should always be used where it is desired to limit the insurance to the personal responsibility of a trustee.

N. Brit. & Mer. Ins. Co. vs. Moffat, L. R., 7 C. B., 25.

Sometimes, too, the trustee is interested by reason of liens or advances made on consignments of goods, and this would be properly expressed by "his interest" in the goods.

Parks vs. Assurance Co., 5 Pick., 34.

Above all, it is important to know just what constitutes a trusteeship in goods as distinguished from an ordinary ownership. About the best test is the right of the consignor to compel a return to him of the specific goods in the hands of another. If this right exists, they are held by the latter in trust ; but if he is only obligated to account for their moneyed value, the consignee is an owner, not a trustee. In the latter case all such goods are covered by an insurance of the consignee as owner, in the former they are only covered by such words as "in trust," or "on commission."

Rice vs. Nixon, *ante*.

The most familiar illustration of this distinction, and one which has occasioned the most litigation, is that of grain in warehouses. Sometimes the grain is delivered purely for purposes of storage, but to avoid the difficulty of keeping each specific lot separate it is understood that the lots may be mingled, but that the consignor is to reclaim an equal quantity of the same grade. This is a mere trusteeship, or bailment, as it is called, on the part of the warehouseman ; the sender of the goods remains the owner and is liable in case of their destruction. Sometimes the warehouseman takes the grain on his own responsibility, agreeing to return a moneyed or some other equivalent. This is a sale, and the warehouseman is the owner. Often, too, it becomes difficult to determine whether the parties intended a sale or a bailment by their agreement; and then the courts will inquire into their intentions and the usages of the business.

Rice vs. Nixon, *ante*, and cases there cited.

Where goods on storage are insured by the owner, they should be insured as "on storage;" otherwise the policy may not always attach, on account of an exempting clause.

In all cases of alleged trusteeships the relation of the trustee to the property should be such as will justify an insurance. Thus a party who was simply renting separate rooms for storage purposes to various parties, and surrendering control of the rooms to them, would have no trust that would justify an insurance of goods stored, unless he had agreed to be responsible for their loss. Executors and administrators should never be allowed to insure in their own names the real estate of the deceased, unless by the will or by the law they are intrusted with its care, and then the insurance should be for the benefit of the heirs or devisees. Sometimes it is willed to them in trust, then they may properly insure as "trustees" or "owners in trust;" but the executor or administrator is in law the owner of the personalty belonging to an unsettled estate, and is the proper party to insure it as "executor."

Common carriers, such as railroad and express companies, form a peculiar class of trustees. The law holds them liable for any damage to property in their care unless it occurs through an act of God. They may limit this liability by a special agreement exempting losses that were unavoidable, but they cannot escape the consequence of such as are due to their own negligence.

Germania Ins. Co. vs. R. R. Co., 7 Ins. Law Jour., 547 ; Steinway vs. R. R. Co., 43 N. Y., 126; Prov.-Washington Ins. Co. vs. The Sidney, 14 Ins. Law Jour., 382.

Carriers, therefore, have an insurable interest in all property in their charge. But since their liability may be restricted by special contract, such risks should be limited to property "for which they may be liable as carrier." Another reason why this limitation should be enforced, is that goods in transit are frequently stored or warehoused with such carriers. If this warehousing is a mere incident in their transportation, it is still a carrier's risk. But if done, for instance, at the end of the route for the accommodation of the shipper when the carrier's duty is ended, it is a mere warehouse risk for which the carrier is not liable, but which would be covered by a simple policy on property "in trust." For the same reason precautions should 'be observed in warehouse risks that are connected with any general transportation system.

The insurance of goods by owners or shippers while in the care of such carriers, too, is fraught with a peculiar danger; for the carrier's bill of lading frequently stipulates that it shall have the benefit of such insurance, and this provision, it has been held, defeats the right of subrogation on the part of the insurer.

Hine & Nichols' Dig., 595—s. c., 117 U. S., 312.

INSURANCE OF PROPERTY NOT THEIR OWN.

The extensive mercantile demand for insurance on personal property belonging to other parties which may be temporarily in the custody of the applicant, justifies a few special words on this subject. All such property, whether it be goods consigned to a commission merchant, deposited in a warehouse in course of transportation on a railroad, or simply in the custody of another awaiting delivery to the owner, is included in the legal term of bailments. But the obligations and responsibilities of custodians may differ very widely, and are regulated by the specific character of the relations of each. Hence, the bailee may in one case have a large insurable interest, while in another, strictly speaking, he may have none at all, and insurance by him may be a mere voluntary act for the owner. But the liberality of the law in permitting a bailee to act for the owner when the circumstances are such as to justify it, even without the express authority of the owner, renders it in all cases important that the actual ownership of the insured property should be stated. A policy simply on "merchandise contained in a store" might cover the interests of a dozen people who were never contemplated by the insurer; such phraseology should never be used; while if on "*his* merchandise," it would be restricted, as was intended, to the property of the insured.

In general, it may be said that any language in such a mercantile policy which indicates an intention to cover other interests than those of the insured, will generally receive the most liberal legal construction that the words and facts will justify. The language will not always be restricted to its rigid technical signification, and in case of ambiguity extrinsic evidence may be admitted to show what was intended by the applicant to be included. Hence, frequent disputes have arisen as to what property was intended in such cases, and great care is needed both in the choice of appropriate language and in ascertaining what interests are to be included when this class of policies is to be written. Reference to a few of the disputed cases will serve best to illustrate this subject. The broad, general principle of the law was thus laid down in Duncan vs. Ins. Co., 12 La. An., 486. The policy insured a railroad on merchandise in certain depots and in transit. Neither ownership nor interest was stated. The policy provided that goods in trust or on commission must be declared. It was held that if, upon a general survey of the policy-conditions and the circumstances, the intention appeared to be to cover an interest not named, such intention would not be defeated for the want of technical or even customary phrases; but it would here seem that only the interest of the railroad was intended, and it must at least show liability for loss of goods belonging to others. It was obvious that the railroad could not have intended simply its own property, and the policy was fatally defective in not stating whose interests were intended.

The case of Home Ins. Co. vs. Warehouse Company (6 Ins. Law Jour., 39) is replete with instructive doctrines sustained by authorities. The insurance was taken out by warehousemen on "merchandise their own, or held by them in trust, or in which they have an interest or liability." It was contended, on the one hand, that only the interest of the warehousemen in the property was intended, and on the other that the policy covered the merchandise itself, regardless of interest. The court declared that if the language of a policy is so ambiguous as to require it, resort may be had to outside evidence to ascertain what was intended. Where it is taken out "for or on account of the owner," or "on account of whom it may concern," outside evidence may thus be taken (a sufficient proof of the faultiness of such language); but here there is nothing ambiguous, the language is as broad as possible, it was the merchandise itself that was covered. If otherwise, says the court, why was not the subject described as the interest of the insured in the merchandise, and not that merchandise itself. The policy covered their own merchandise, together with that in which they had any interest or liability, and also any merchandise which they held in trust. The last phrase in insurance policies does not mean property held technically as trustees, but in the mercantile sense of goods intrusted to them by their customers. As warehousemen they had liens for charges, expenses, advances, and commissions, which could all be specifically insured under their interest. They could also insure in their own names for their customers as well as themselves, as in the present instance, and recover the full value of the goods. It further appeared that the depositors had independently insured their own property. This was held to be other insurance, and the company was compelled to contribute. It would be difficult to find the objections to this omnibus style of writing more completely summed up than in this single decision.

This right to insure the property of others in their possession, regardless of liability or authority from the owners, is liberally extended by the law to other classes in the mercantile community. In Waring vs. Ins. Co. it was extended in the case of a policy on goods "their own or sold but not removed" to property which had been sold and paid for but not taken away for the benefit not simply of the original purchasers, but of successive owners, though not designated, and without previous authority. The court distinguished the phrase from "sold but not delivered," which referred to goods where the ownership had not changed for want of technical delivery. In Stillwell vs. Staples (19 N. Y., 401) insurance on property held in trust included cloth left with a manufacturer to be made into clothing without any previous orders to insure. But where the policy was on goods "in trust," in which the nature of such trust was explained before insuring, in Parks vs. Ass'e Co. (5 Pick., 34), the insurance was restricted to the interest as understood. So, where the policy specifically requires that property so held shall be stated, as in Rafael vs. Ins. Co. (7 La. An., 244), the provision must generally be complied with. In Stillwell vs. Staples (19 N. Y., 401), a party insuring his own and goods in trust was allowed to elect whether the insurance should apply solely to his own or not. In Ætna Ins. Co. vs. Jackson (16 B. Mon., 250) the policy was on "all the articles making up the stock of a pork-house, and all within the building and pertinent thereto." This sweeping description of the contents of a risk like a pork-house was held to override a special clause requiring goods on commission to be insured as such, and to cover everything that could be included in the description, regardless of ownership."

It will be seen from these cases how completely the aim of the insurer to restrict the policy to the interests of the party insured may be defeated in this class of policies by failing to clearly designate the interests which were intended to be covered. Every additional interest which can be loaded on such a policy in case of partial loss, is an added liability for which there was no corresponding increase of premium. Agents will take notice and avoid general and ambiguous terms, as well as blanket forms, in policy-writing.

MORTGAGES, JUDGMENTS, AND OTHER LIENS.

A lien of any kind against property, to be insurable, should be specific in its character. An ordinary creditor has no right to insure the property of a debtor unless he has some special claim upon that particular property as security for the debt, though this claim need not necessarily be a strictly legal lien.

Ross vs. Merch. Ins. Co., 27 La., 409 ; Rohrbach vs. Germania Ins. Co., 4 Ins. Law Jour., 737.

But it is safer and better in almost all cases to restrict insurances of this kind to such liens as will follow the property in any attempted transfer of ownership. Such are the liens of factors and commission merchants for advances or charges in connection with goods in their possession, of judgment-creditors, and especially of mortgagees. In all cases of this kind, where the legal title vests in another, the insurance for a creditor should be on "his interest" as mortgagee, etc. The better rule, however, in the case of all liens where the property is not actually in the possession of the mortgagee or other lien-holder, is to insure only the legal owner and protect the mortgagee by making the loss payable to him as his interest may appear. Not only is the danger of excessive insurance on the property by two separate interests thus avoided, but another important object is gained. The party insured is the one who is responsible for any violation of the policy-conditions, he is the party with whom the contract is made, and should obviously, if possible, be the one who is in control of the property.

Sias vs. Ins. Co., 9 Ins. Law Jour., 154, and cases there cited.

Most important among these liens, and those which have occasioned most controversy in the courts, are mortgage-interests in real estate. The law permits the mortgagor to insure the property to its full value, regardless of incumbrance, and the mortgagee or other lien-holder to insure to the extent of his interest. Indeed, the latter has sometimes been allowed, without stating the nature of his interest, to also insure and recover the full value of the property. It is important, therefore, that all separate insurance of mortgagees should be limited to their interest as such.

Columbian Ins. Co. vs. Lawrence, 10 Pet., 507; Ins. Co. vs. Updegraff, 9 Harris, 513.

In nearly all the States, however, except Massachusetts, the companies are protected against the ultimate payment of more than the actual amount of damages by the doctrine of subrogation, which allows them to demand an assignment of the lien for their own benefit upon the payment of its full amount to the lien-holder, if the latter is the party insured.

Kernochen vs. Ins. Co., 17 N. Y., 428 ; Ætna Ins. Co. vs. Tyler, 16 Wend., 385.

Where the owner is insured solely for his own benefit without reference to any claims of mortgagees, the latter have no rights in his policy. The former may retain the whole insurance money, though the lien covers the whole moneyed value of the property. The opportunity thus given for fraud will suggest the propriety of making such policies payable to mortgagees to the extent of their interest, unless the interest of the owner is largely in excess of the insurance.

Stearns vs. Ins. Co., 7 Ins. Law Jour., 506, and cases there cited. .

But mortgages usually provide that the mortgagor shall insure for the benefit of the mortgagee, and where such appears to have been the intention of the parties the courts will enforce it.

Cromwell vs. Ins. Co., 44 N. Y., 42.

If a policy is simply made payable to a mortgagee or to any other party, without limiting the amount of payment, the party named may be allowed by the court to collect the whole sum, irrespective of interest, leaving the insured to compel a repayment of the excess. Therefore, indorsements of payments to lien-holders should be limited to their interests as such.

Goodall vs. Ins. Co., 25 N. H., 169.

The great advantage of policies which thus insure the owner directly, with loss payable to other parties as their interest may appear, is that the owner's interests as well as the others, are protected. Whatever the mortgagee receives will cancel by so much the mortgage-debt, while the balance goes to the owner. Such is not usually the case where the mortgagee or lien-holder is the insured party. The owner here has no interest. The company, by paying its amount, is entitled to receive and enforce the mortgage against him.

Parties to whom policies are thus made payable have no other rights under the contract than that of receiving the money, if the company is obligated to pay at all. The insured may surrender the policy, and to prevent this the mortgagee usually keeps the instrument; or he may render it void by violating its conditions, or the company may elect to replace or repair the property, in which case no moneyed damages are payable. -

Brunswick Savings Inst. vs. Ins. Co., 8 Ins. Law Jour., 120, and cases there cited ; Heilman vs. Ins. Co., 8 Ins. Law Jour., 53; Stamps vs. Ins. Co., 7 Ins. Law Jour., 256.

To avoid the danger of having the policy avoided by acts of the insured, many mortgagees, especially corporations, insist on what are known as mortgage-clauses being attached to the policies, stipulating in effect that, if thus forfeited as to the interest of the mortgagor, they shall remain valid as to the mortgagee. The effect of such a clause in case of violation by the mortgagor is to convert the policy into a direct insurance of the mortgagee, under a contract wholly independent of the mortgagor.

Five Cents Savings Bank vs. Ins. Co., 6 Ins. Law Jour., 437 ; Meriden Savings Bank vs. Ins. Co., 12 Ins. Law Jour., 620.

The original insured is thus released from all obligations in respect to the premises. In case of such independent insurance of the mortgagee, the company, upon the payment of the mortgage, is usually subrogated to his rights against the mortgagor. In case of other insurance by the latter, no contribution can be compelled. Replacement can only be effected with the consent of the mortgagor in possession.

Ulster Savings Inst. vs. Decker, 7 Ins. Law Jour., 859 ; Foster vs. Van Reed, 8 Ins. Law Jour., 201 ; Ætna Ins. Co. vs. Baker, 10 Ins. Law Jour., 253 ; Bank vs. Ins. Co., 9 Ins. Law Jour., 928.

Though in practice, where other insurance by the mortgagor exists, the companies are usually able by co-operation to effect a single settlement of the loss, either by a single money payment or replacement, the attachment of such mortgage-clauses is strongly objected to by many of them, because they thus release all parties from responsibility for the care of the property or the truthfulness of the representations on which the insurance has been secured. The same objections, of course, attach to insurance directly on the interest of the mortgagee, judgment-creditor, or other lien-holder. In Conn. Fire Ins. Co. vs. Ins. Co. (15 Ins. Law Jour., 895) the property was independently insured by the owner, the mortgagee, and the lessee ; it was replaced by the insurer of the latter, and the court ruled that no contribution could be collected from the other insurers, since they were on different interests.

In regard to all clauses stipulating for a payment of the insurance money to another than the party insured, it should be remembered that insurance is in its nature a personal contract, that the question of moral hazard largely enters, and the companies attach no less importance to the parties interested than to the property. For these reasons everything that gives it an impersonal character should be avoided. The law regards such language as "payable to whom it may concern," or "as interest may appear at time of loss," without naming a party, or to a party named regardless of interest, somewhat as a check payable to bearer. Any person answering the description would be entitled to the money. Where it is possible to do so, therefore, both the particular party and his interest should be stated.

Wood on Ins., Sec. 282, and cases there cited.

CAUTION TO AGENTS.

The caution to agents is repeated to keep within the limits of their authority and the known or presumed usages or rules of their companies. Several of the foregoing pages have been written as a warning against the classes of risks described rather than as instructions how to write them. In all cases of this sort the safe plan is to correspond with the company, and only act upon specific instructions in each particular case.

INCIDENTS CONNECTED WITH THE TITLE.

CHANGE OF TITLE OR INTEREST.*

As has been said, a permanent transfer of all his insurable interest by the insured to another party will, of itself, forfeit the policy unless the company also consents to transfer his rights under the policy. Such a transfer by the insured is what is known as an alienation. If the alienation is only temporary, however, and the interest is re-transferred before the loss occurs, the policy will again attach.

Young vs. Ins. Co., 14 Gray, 150 ; Baldwin vs. Ins. Co., 10 Ins. Law Jour., 32 ; Hitchcock vs. Ins. Co., 26 N. Y., 68.

But there are many changes in the nature and extent of the interest of the insured which fall short of a complete alienation, which leave him with perhaps only a very limited interest in the property, but yet which would be sufficient in law to sustain an insurance. To protect against such changes, special prohibitions are inserted in policies against any change of title or possession. The thing prohibited by such clauses is the transfer to other parties of the legal rights of the insured, whether in respect to the ownership or control. An incumbrance is not a change of title, nor is a mere agreement to sell, if the actual sale has not taken place. So it has been held that involuntary transfers through the action of the law, such as seizure and sale by the sheriff, are not what is intended by the language of the policy, unless specifically included in the prohibition.

Baldwin vs. Ins. Co., 10 Ins. Law Jour., 32 ; Keeney vs. Ins. Co., 7 Ins. Law Jour., 100 ; Browning vs. Ins. Co., 7 Ins. Law Jour., 428 ; Appleton Iron Co. vs. Ins. Co., 46 Wis., 23 ; Jackson vs. Ins. Co., 23 Pick., 418 ; Byers vs. Ins. Co., 9 Ins. Law Jour., 743 ; Sherwood vs. Ins. Co., 73 N. Y., 447.

---

* NOTE.—As a matter of practice the agent should, as far as possible, keep himself advised of all changes of title to or interest in property covered by his policies. When he ascertains that a change has occurred he should do one of two things at once. (1.) If the change brings in a man or men who would be acceptable, persons whom he would insure as readily, and on the same terms, as the original parties, he should promptly make the necessary indorsement on the policy and report the same to the company. (2.) If, however, the change brings in people whom he would not insure, he should just as promptly cancel the policy and return it to the home office. Scrutiny should also be exercised to ascertain whether such changes indicate adversity, embarrassment, removal, speculative experiment, or anything else which might result in reduced value of property or increased moral hazard, and, if these signs should be observed, cancelment should promptly follow.

The effect of a transfer of a part of the insured property has been held by some of the courts to vitiate the whole policy, while by others a distinction has been made between those cases where the insurance is for a single amount on the whole and those where it is apportioned among different items, the policy being still held good as to such items as have not been alienated. So it has been disputed whether a transfer from one partner to another is within the prohibition, where the insurance is to the firm, and the prevailing opinion is that it is not. But where the transfer is made to a new partner, who was not a member of the original firm, the prevailing opinion is that this constitutes a change of title.

Hinman vs. Ins. Co., 48 Wis., 36 ; Baldwin vs. Ins. Co., *supra ;* Card vs. Ins. Co., Hine & Nichols' Dig., 74 ; Hoffman vs. Ins. Co., 33 N. Y., 405.

In all such questions, however, the answer will largely depend on the precise wording of the policy, the court favoring such a construction as will support the insurance if any insurable interest exists. For this reason the prohibition is often extended in the policy to cover all changes which reduce the insurable interest; whether by incumbrance, legal process, or judicial decree, whether in whole or in part, voluntary or involuntary. The safe rule, therefore, for the insured is to make no conveyance or transfer and impose or suffer no lien upon the property, whether voluntary or involuntary, without duly notifying the company and securing its consent.

All assignments of policies from one owner to another should be executed on the regular assignment-blanks furnished for the purpose. The signature should be that of the owner himself, the duty of the agent is limited to indorsing consent. An agent has no more right to transfer a policy from one owner to another by an *ex parte* indorsement, than to transfer any other contract. His authority is restricted to giving consent for the company. All indorsements, of whatever kind, which he may be called on to make, the agent should sign personally in writing as agent. Another important precaution to be noted in this connection is that policy-forms should never be signed in blank, for they might be surreptitiously filled in by other parties and the company made liable.

INCUMBRANCE.

The effect of incumbrances in reducing the interest of the owner is so obvious that the question whether the property is incumbered is one of the most important in the application, and the prohibition against incumbrance one of the most important in the policy. False answers in the one case, and violations in the other, are prominent among the grounds on which loss-payments have been refused by the companies. Any valid.

lien which attaches especially against the property, that is, which would follow the property if transferred to another party, should be regarded as an incumbrance, whether it be in the shape of a mortgage, tax-lien, attachment, judgment, dower right, mechanics' lien, or any specific legal obligation whatever imposed on the property to respond to the demands of another. This is the safe rule, for it is difficult to determine in some cases just what will be deemed an incumbrance within the policy. The mere rental of property, however, for a term of years, is not treated as an incumbrance.

Fuller vs. Ins. Co., 4 Ins. Law Jour., 841 ; Baley vs. Ins. Co., 9 Ins. Law Jour., 187 ; Redmond vs. Ins. Co., 10 Ins. Law Jour., 287 ; Ohio Ins. Co. vs. Britton, 7 Ins. Law Jour., 632 ; Lockwood vs. Ins. Co., 11 Ins. Law Jour., 40.

In all cases, therefore, where insurance is applied for, inquiry should be made, not simply whether the property is mortgaged or pledged, but whether other parties are interested, or have claims or rights of any kind in respect to it ; and if it appears doubtful whether a lien or claim would be deemed an incumbrance, let the fact of its existence be stated in the application and in the policy, if called for. The validity of the policy will be governed, not by what the applicant may think to be an incumbrance, but what the law so regards. If more than one incumbrance exists, all should be stated, together with their character and the amount of each. Let the company be the judge of their importance. Failures in this respect have been the cause of repeated forfeitures.

Lowell vs. Ins. Co., 8 Cush., 127 ; Masters vs. Ins. Co., 11 Barb., 624 ; Wilbur vs. Ins. Co., 10 Cush., 446.

If no stipulation is made regarding subsequent incumbrances, an incumbrance imposed on the property after the insurance has been granted will not affect the validity of the policy. But the policy generally provides that it shall be void, also, in the case of subsequent incumbrance without consent first obtained from the company. Such knowledge and consent, therefore, are as important in this case as before. The courts uniformly hold that in either case a concealment of the facts by the insured, when thus called for by the application or policy, will vitiate the insurance.

Redmond vs. Ins. Co., 10 Ins. Law Jour., 287, and cases there cited ; Supple vs. Ins. Co., 11 Ins. Law Jour., 782 ; Indiana Ins. Co. vs. Brehm, 12 Ins. Law Jour., 607, and cases there cited ; Ellis vs. Ins. Co., 12 Ins. Law Jour., 895.

While, as has been said, an incumbrance is not of itself a change of title, it frequently results in such change, or even complete alienation, through foreclosure. The company, therefore, should be promptly notified of foreclosure or any other legal proceedings, such as insolvency, calculated to affect the ownership.

Keeney vs. Ins. Co., 7 Ins. Law Jour., 100; Strong vs. Ins. Co., 10 Pick., 40; Ayres vs. Ins. Co., 17 Iowa, 180.

The death of the insured has also in some cases been held to be a change of title and a ground of forfeiture, though policies are usually good to the heirs. So the dissolution of a partnership may terminate a policy to partners. The company should consequently be notified in either case, and proper indorsements secured if it should appear desirable to continue the insurance.

Keeney vs. Ins. Co., 3 T. & C., 478; Dreher vs. Ins. Co., 18 Mo., 128; Burbank vs. Ins. Co., 24 N. H., 550; Lappin vs. Ins. Co., 58 Barb., 325.

Another important point regarding changes in the interest of the insured, whether affecting his title or in the shape of incumbrances, is that unless the agent is on his guard a renewal of the insurance where such changes are known by the agent may result in waiving the forfeiture of the policy.

Hay vs. Ins. Co., 8 Ins. Law Jour., 633; Aurora Ins. Co. vs. Kranich, 6 Ins. Law Jour., 676.

The law regards all incumbrances which seriously affect the moneyed interest of the insured in the property as of vital importance, and any failure to correctly state such facts as are called for is *prima facie* evidence of bad faith. A man may be ignorant of law and thus state inaccurately the nature of his title, and the law will look leniently on such cases; but a failure to disclose a lien which seriously reduces the value of the property to him is looked on as a plain breach of faith.

The practical point to the agent in all this detail is to show him how easily a company may become involved in difficulty through his ignorance or inadvertance, and to emphasize the well-known rules of the best companies to keep off or to get off from property which is too heavily mortgaged, to drop men who get into embarrassed and desperate circumstances, and to avoid complicated ownerships; all these things tend toward incendiarism and fraud, and are productive of loss to the companies.

VALUATION OF INSURED PROPERTY.

Under the ordinary open policy the amount to be recovered in case of loss is always limited in law to the measure of actual damages, no matter how much may be insured, except in those States where the valued-policy law is in force. But in spite of this legal limitation, and in spite of the fact that the company may, by replacement, protect itself against attempted extortion, the opportunities for concealment and fraud are so numerous, and the difficulty of securing a fair estimate of the damage after a loss has often proved so great, that overinsurance has become the recognized bane of the business, and is a danger against which the agent should ever be on his guard. Wherever the valued-policy law exists, the sum insured in case of total loss becomes the measure of liability, no matter what the actual value of the building may be, nor what stipulations to the contrary may be made between the parties.

· Queen Ins. Co. vs. Ice Co., 15 Ins. Law Jour., 109; Reilly vs. Ins. Co., 7 Ins. Law Jour., 391, and cases there cited.

Under this law a peculiar responsibility rests upon the agent. Negligence on his part in permitting excessive insurance may impose an excessive loss upon his company, of which judicial cognizance could be taken as it could not ordinarily be where the law limits recovery to the actual amount lost, and there is no sound reason in such a case why the agent could not be compelled to respond to his company in damages. In the absence of such a law, the injury which may be done is not confined to the risk of assessing excessive damages, but may prevent the company from taking advantage of a manifest attempt at fraud. This was illustrated in the case of Dupree vs. Ins. Co. (14 Ins. Law Jour., 57). It was claimed that the insured had forfeited all right of recovery by fixing a knowingly false and fraudulent value in the application; the answer was, that the property had been examined and valued by the agent, and the answer was justified by the court.

A fraudulent overvaluation of his property by the insured when applying for insurance will forfeit the policy if it can be conclusively proved, and a grossly excessive valuation will be treated as evidence tending to prove a fraud. But the mere fact of the valuation being thus excessive will not, as a matter of law, be treated as conclusively fraudulent, though under special stipulations in the contract, the simple fact of a gross excess has been allowed to defeat the policy. While, therefore, dishonesty is discouraged by the law, the latter must not be depended on to prevent it.

Franklin Ins. Co. vs. Vaughan, 2 Otto, 516; Sidney vs. Ins. Co., 8 Ins. Law Jour., 461; Citizens' Ins. Co. vs. Short, 8 Ins. Law Jour., 126; Boutelle vs. Ins. Co., 7 Ins. Law Jour., 781.

The agent's judgment as to values for insurance purposes should be governed by the same commercial principles which the law applies in case of loss. This is in all cases the cash value at the time and place; that is, the amount of cash down which would be the commercial equivalent of the property. The meaning of this term will be more clearly understood when it is contrasted with what is not a correct measure of value. It is not what the thing may be worth to the owner, but what others would give for it. This was well illustrated in the case of Niblo vs. Ins. Co. (1 Sandf., 551), where the insurance was on a leasehold interest in which by reason of the circumstances the insured had a special interest, but the court held that the true question was, "How much would a stranger, having no contracts pending, have given for the unexpired lease?" The cost of replacing the subject of insurance should rarely be regarded as a correct measure of value. Ordinarily, this involves the substitution of new for old, which would manifestly be unjust. Frequently it involves the replacement of a subject whose commercial value would not equal the cost of producing it. An antiquated machine might be very complicated, and require a heavy outlay to reproduce, whereas the introduction of a newer and cheaper substitute or a change in the method of manufacturing may have rendered it of little value. Manufactured articles may have been expensive to create, but something newer has taken their place, their commercial value has gone. For these reasons the cost of reproduction or replacement is seldom recognized by the courts as of itself a fair test of value.

Hoffman vs. Ins. Co., 1 La. An., 216; Ætna Ins. Co. vs. Johnson, 11 Bush., 587; Commercial Ins. Co. vs. Sennett, 37 Penn. St., 205; Carson vs. Ins. Co., 2 Wash., 468.

When the subject of insurance is of a kind that has a ready market-sale, as in the case of ordinary merchandise, the cash market-value is the legal value. But here again the agent must be on his guard. The retail price of merchandise in stock is by no means what insurers nor even the courts in all cases regard as its value. That price includes the profit of the seller, which is no part of the subject of insurance. The question is, what are they worth as a whole, and in the place where they are to parties wishing to purchase? In the case of manufacturers and others as well, the question should be narrowed down still farther; they may be able to replace the stock at less than an outsider would be willing to give for it, so that here the legal rule would allow an insurance of profits. For insurance purposes, therefore, the value should never be regarded as more than the actual cost to the insured of replacement. And since the companies are rarely willing to insure the full estimated value, and since the value, too, is likely to be depreciated, this figure should be taken simply as a gauge from which a proper reduction is to be made. In the case of property which may have a ready sale, but is not of a merchantable character, such as household goods, the safe rule is to treat it as worth no more than it would bring at auction.

Marchesseau vs. Ins. Co., 1 Rob., La., 438; Hercules Ins. Co. vs. Hunter, 14 C. C.

S., 1,137 ; Fowler vs. Ins Co., 6 Ins. Law Jour., 432 ; Murphrey vs. Ins. Co., 5 Ins. Law Jour., 297.

Buildings having no ready sale, and being of little value apart from the land on which they stand, are subject to a different rule. The law estimates the value of a building on the same principle as does a purchaser who first fixes on what the ground is worth, and then how much in addition should be allowed for the building. Its age, utility, general condition, and cost of construction or replacement, may all furnish aid towards framing a judgment, but its cost or the cost of replacement is by no means the correct measure of its worth.

Brinley vs. Ins. Co., 11 Met., 195 ; Ætna Ins. Co. vs. Johnson, *ante*.

In practice this legal rule has been found to be extremely favorable to the insured, allowing damages to be assessed by a jury without any fixed basis, and often in fact computed on the cost of restoring. The law has refused, also, to recognize the fact that a building whose speedy removal is compelled, or whose restoration, if damaged, the law will not permit, is on that account any the less valuable, though it may be practically worthless.

Bayly vs. Ins. Co., 4 Ins. Law Jour., 503 ; Collingridge vs. Royal Exchange, Q. B. L. R., 3 Q. B. D.; Brady vs. Ins. Co., 11 Mich., 425 ; Brown vs. Ins. Co., 1 E. & E., 853.

The legal rule as to buildings, therefore, is not always a safe guide for the agent, even as a standard from which to estimate, since it sometimes enables the insured to dispose of his property to the company at a fictitious price, or rid himself of property otherwise unsalable. In addition to the actual worth as commonly estimated, the agent should closely scan the rental value and treat with the utmost caution buildings that are unprofitable, liable to removal, or which if seriously damaged could not be repaired on account of building laws. All such should be insured for much less than what would otherwise be their apparent worth, or should be declined in toto. The safe rule, aside from all legalties, is to insure only such property as is valuable to the owner, and then never to insure it for such an amount or in such a manner as to render the insurance of more value than the property.

OTHER INSURANCE.

The same reasons which lead the companies to restrict the amount of insurance which they are willing to grant upon property, lead them also to insist that additional insurance shall not be taken out in other companies, without their consent. The policy-prohibition against other insurance is grounded upon the danger of overinsurance and consequent fraud. There is another important reason, too, for this requirement. In case of loss the contributing liability of each insurer is affected by the conditions as well as amounts of other policies, and since additional insurance to a limited amount may frequently be an advantage by reducing the liability, a stipulation that a certain amount of insurance shall be maintained is also sometimes added. The force of these reasons is fully recognized by the courts, and a violation of the stipulations regarding other insurance, unless waived, will result in the penalty being enforced, which is generally forfeiture.

Kennedy vs. Ins. Co., 6 Ins. Law Jour., 359; Behler vs. Ins. Co., 9 Ins. Law Jour., 798; Phœnix Ins. Co. vs. Stevenson, 8 Ins. Law Jour., 922; Pitney vs. Ins. Co., 4 Ins. Law Jour., 765.

Every insurance, however, on the same property is not recognized by the courts as other insurance, and the object aimed at by the companies is thus often defeated. Not only must the insurance cover the same subject-matter, but the same interest. In the case of City Savings Bank vs. Ins. Co. (6 Ins. Law Jour., 437) the property was insured by the owner, and afterwards a mortgagee obtained insurance independently on his own interest. This was held not to be other insurance within the meaning of the first policy, it was on a wholly different interest. So, in Wheeler vs. Ins. Co. (10 Ins. Law Jour., 354), a policy for his benefit was taken out by the owner of the property, and another policy was secured independently by the mortgagee. This was declared not to be a case of other insurance. The policies were on separate interests.

See also Jackson vs. Ins. Co., 23 Pick., 418; Thomas vs. Ins. Co., 119 Mass., 121; Harris vs. Ins. Co., 5 Ohio, 467. Also what is said *ante* concerning mortgage interests.

But the mere fact that one of the policies is payable to another party, will not amount to separate interests if the interest and the party insured are the same. In Pitney vs. Ins. Co. (4 Ins. Law Jour., 765) the owner, who held a policy payable to himself, afterwards procured another, payable as interest should appear to another. This was not insurance of a separate interest, and was held to be a violation.

Again, it is not always easy to determine whether the double insurance is strictly on the same subject-matter where the policies are not concurrent, and the courts are not agreed how far non-concurrency will affect the question. In Sloat vs. Ins. Co. (49 Pa. St., 14) one policy covered the building, while another covered the building, machinery, tools, etc., and it was held not to be a case of fatal double insurance within the policy. So, in Balt. Ins. Co. vs. Loney (20 Md., 20), a policy on merchants' goods and another on his own goods and those held on commission were held not to be double insurances. On the other hand, in Walton vs. Ins. Co. (2 Rob., La., 563), goods which were insured in one store were afterwards removed to another, in which was a stock of goods whose insurance under another policy was by its terms extended to the added stock; this was held to be a double insurance. In Ramsay Co. vs. Ins. Co. (11 U. C., Q. B., 516) one policy insured on building and machinery, and the other on these and the stock. This was held to be a double insurance. In short, it may be said that strict concurrency is not always essential to constitute other insurance, a partial concurrency may be enough to violate the condition.

Another and the principal legal difficulty in deciding whether there has been other insurance, arises from the existence of similar or nearly similar clauses in both policies, making them void in such case. Here, again, the decisions have been conflicting. In some cases it has been held that where the one policy is rendered void by the procurement of another in violation of its terms, there is no other insurance within the meaning of the second policy. In other cases, however, it has been held that the first policy was not actually void, but only voidable; that other insurance therefore existed ; and where the policy expressly forbids other insurance even though void, such other insurance will work a forfeiture.

Phœnix Ins. Co. vs. Lamar, 15 Ins. Law Jour., 686 ; Stevenson vs. Ins. Co., 14 Ins. Law Jour., 65; Behrens vs. Ins. Co., 13 Ins. Law Jour., 492; Gee vs. Ins. Co., 4 Ins. Law Jour., 489; Southerland vs. Ins. Co., 8 Ins. Law Jour., 181, and cases there cited.

The clear intention of the underwriters has in these various ways repeatedly been defeated by the courts. Attention should be directed, therefore, not simply to the question whether there is other insurance beyond a legal quibble, but whether the property is covered either in whole or in part by another policy, no matter in whose interest it may be issued. As has been already noted, one of the chief objections to the insurance of merely equitable and limited interests, such as those of a mortgagee, arises from the probability of other insurance, which cannot be compelled to contribute in case of loss. Another precaution which should be observed, is that in case of other insurance the policies should be made as nearly as possible concurrent, that is, one policy should not be made general or floating as to two or more items where the other insures specific sums on each, a matter which is explained more fully under " Concurrency in Writing."

But the misconduct, or alleged misconduct, of the agent, more than any other cause, has been instrumental in defeating the prohibition against other insurance, through his waiver of the stipulation. The policy usually stipulates for notice and the indorsement of a written consent in case of other insurance. But notice is generally received and the indorsement made by an authorized agent. Unless there be some express provision in the policy to the contrary, the law regards the agent who is authorized to write the policy as the proper party to give the consent, and his verbal acquiescence, or even knowledge at the time of contracting, has repeatedly been treated as a waiver of the written indorsement. In New Orleans Ass'n vs. Griffen (15 Ins. Law Jour., 303) verbal consent of such an agent, with knowledge that it would be acted on, was held to be a waiver. In Kitchen vs. Ins. Co. (14 Ins. Law Jour., 594) and in Security Ins. Co. vs. Fay (22 Mich., 467) it was held that the acquiescence of the mere solicitor in the obtaining of other insurance was sufficient under the circumstances to estop the company from setting up the policy-violation ; and while the ordinary rule requires the agent to be one authorized to grant insurances, these cases serve to show the dangerous results which may flow from the conduct, even of a solicitor, where the application itself contains no provision on the subject. Ordinarily, notice of other insurance to a solicitor is not notice to the company.

Heath vs. Ins. Co., 58 N. H. See also Collins vs. Ins. Co., 8 Ins. Law Jour., 453; Roberts vs. Ins. Co., 6 Ins. Law Jour., 248; Westchester Ins. Co. vs. Earle, 5 Ins. Law Jour., 61; Pechner vs. Ins. Co., 4 Ins. Law Jour., 782, and cases there cited.

The agent, therefore, cannot be too careful when he has knowledge of other insurance, either subsisting or intended. Mere silence or inaction on his part may serve to defeat the policy-provision. The insured should be promptly informed that consent must be indorsed, and until the indorsement is made, the consent should be withheld.

Schenck vs. Ins. Co., 24 N. J., 447; Hayward vs. Ins. Co., 2 Ins. Law Jour., 503; Viele vs. Ins. Co., 26 Iowa, 55.

One class of cases in this connection calls for a separate notice. The agent frequently acts for more than one company, and distributes the risk among them, or, when it is objected to by one, cancels the policy and places it in another. Failure to act in accordance with strict business principles under such circumstances has occasioned no little litigation. From the very nature of the case, the agent has knowledge of the other insurance in respect to each policy, and a failure to indorse it will not defeat the contract, though the applicant neglects on his part to mention the fact in his application.

Brandup vs. Ins. Co., 10 Ins. Law Jour., 228, and cases there cited.

So, in regard to cancellation and transfer of the risk, the agent should remember that even though free to elect the company in the first place, after having once elected and made a binding contract in one, he is not thereafter free to shift the risk to another, except in the manner stipulated in the contract by due notice to the insured and cancellation of the first policy, and when so canceled and the consent of the insured obtained, it should be promptly bound in the second company. -

Poor vs. Ins. Co., 9 Ins. Law Jour., 428; Ætna Ins. Co. vs. Maguire, 51 Ill., 342.

VACANCY.

Few questions have occasioned more controversy in the courts than vacancy. All policies expressly stipulate against it. In the case of special hazards particular inquiries are usually made on this subject. The reason is obvious. Vacant buildings have always furnished the strongest temptation for the malicious incendiary's torch. A violation of the policy-provision against vacancy is uniformly admitted to be a breach of contract which will work a forfeiture ; the vital question has been as to what constituted such vacancy. Often the premises are described as "occupied as a residence" or "occupied by tenants." Such statements, while they must be true as regards existing conditions, are not in themselves warranties that the occupancy shall continue, and should never be relied on for that purpose.

Hartford Ins. Co. vs. Smith, 7 Ins. Law Jour., 140 ; Woodruff vs. Ins. Co., 10 Ins. Law Jour., 125 ; Imperial Ins. Co. vs. Kiernan, 15 Ins. Law Jour., 352.

Every temporary non-occupancy of a building or of insured premises is not regarded as a vacancy by the courts. The question depends upon the language of the prohibition and the character of the risk, as well as the extent and duration of the abandonment. Thus in Cummings vs. Ins. Co. (6 Ins. Law Jour., 135) a distinction was made between an ordinary provision against vacancy and one that provided against a vacancy by the removal of the occupant, which latter referred only to a permanent abandonment. A dwelling is assumed to be continuously occupied as a place of residence. When it fails to comply with this description, it is vacant. Frequently the house is closed for a longer or shorter time, through the temporary absence of the family for a brief sojourn elsewhere ; the courts will not always regard such absences as a policy-violation, especially if a servant remains on the premises. But any prolonged absence and closing of a dwelling is liable to be fatal to the insurance. The mere fact of occasional visits or of a general supervision by some person in the neighborhood is not sufficient. All cases where a residence is thus vacated for any length of time should be treated as a case of va-

cancy for which consent must be obtained. Thus in Ins. Co. vs. Race
(15 Ins. Law Jour., 633) it appeared that while the owner was temporarily absent his wife abandoned the dwelling and himself. It appeared
that the house was frequently visited by members of the family for the
purpose of looking after the furniture, and a servant generally slept there
at night, but there were no fires lighted nor any of the usual signs of occupancy. This was held by the court to be a violation of the policy.
So in Herman vs. Ins. Co. (10 Ins. Law Jour., 743) a summer residence,
which was annually occupied during the season, was looked after by a servant
and his family, who lived in an adjacent house on the same grounds, but it
was held to be vacant within the policy. In Ins. Co. vs. Padfield (78 Ill.,
167) the court said with regard to this condition : "A fair and reasonable
construction of the language vacant and unoccupied is that it should be
without an occupant, without any person living in it ; not technical occupation, but as popularly understood and used." The mere presence
of furniture, therefore, coupled with a general oversight, should not be
regarded as an occupancy in case of a building used for dwelling purposes.

The question of vacancy in this class of risks is most likely to arise
through an abandonment by the tenant or a change of tenancy, when an
interval longer or shorter is apt to occur during which the property is not
occupied. There is considerable disagreement between the courts as to
the effect of such changes and removals. Where the property is known
to be used for renting, and where the owner is ignorant of the abandonment, they are disposed to be more lenient. The language of the policy,
too, will have much to do in deciding the question. A provision that it
shall not be and remain unoccupied would be looked on as excusing
such a brief vacancy as was incidental to a change of tenants. A provision, on the contrary, restricting the vacancy to five days would be regarded as absolute. The safe and proper rule is to regard the property
as vacant the moment it ceases to be occupied by parties living on the
premises, no matter how brief the non-occupancy. The fact that another
tenant is preparing to occupy, or that an effort is being made to secure
such a tenant, or even that a portion of the furniture has been placed in
the house, should not be regarded as an occupancy. Thus in American
Ins. Co. vs. Padfield (4 Ins. Law Jour., 893) the tenant had left, but a
few articles of furniture remained, and it was held that mere legal possession was not occupancy. In Ætna Ins. Co. vs. Meyer (8 Ins. Law
Jour., 249) the tenants had left four days previous, but others were to move
in as soon as repairs were completed. But it was held that even a temporary vacancy forfeited the policy. In Dennison vs. Ins. Co. (9 Ins. Law

Jour., 65) a tenant, whose lease had not expired, moved out about two weeks before the fire ; and in McClure vs. Ins. Co. the tenant had moved without the knowledge of the insured, who, immediately upon learning of the fact, sought to secure another tenant, but in neither case was the vacancy held to be excused. In Bennett vs. Ins. Co. (12 Ins. Law Jour., 569) the tenant had moved out only two hours before the fire, but it was held to be a case of vacancy. In other cases the courts have been more liberal.

See also Cook vs. Ins. Co., 9 Ins. Law Jour., 887 ; Kelley vs. Ins. Co., 5 Ins. Law Jour., 134 ; Cummins vs. Ins. Co., 6 Ins. Law Jour., 135.

On the other hand, if the risk is of a character which involves only the presence of persons at stated times or intervals, or only an occasional employment for special purposes, the term occupancy has a very different meaning. Such a building is occupied while in a general sense in use in the manner contemplated. A barn intended simply for storing grain in winter, or a smoke-house for curing at certain seasons, is not vacant because it is not in active use at another season of the year. But it is obvious that the mere term "barn" would not suggest to the underwriter such an occasional use ; therefore, all risks of this character, whose names do not import technical vacancies, should be particularly described as occupied only in such a way. In Ashworth vs. Ins. Co. (112 Mass., 423) the insurance was on a dwelling and a barn on the premises, and the court said that occupancy as applied to such buildings implies such use of the barn as is ordinarily incident to a barn belonging to an occupied house, or at least something more than for mere storage. In a recent case before the Supreme Court of Iowa, the subject of insurance was a hog-house, which had not been used for that purpose, however, for some time. The owner lived in his house near by, and it did not appear that there had been any actual abandonment of the use. The court held that there was no vacancy, though the fact that it was temporarily unused probably increased the risk. In Williams vs. Ins. Co. (14 Ins. Law Jour., 708) an elevator had been sold under foreclosure, the property was idle at the time of fire, but for years it had only been used at irregular intervals, but men were around there all the time, and there was no evidence of an intention to abandon its use as an elevator. Under these circumstances the court held that it was not vacant. In both of these latter cases dispute would have been obviated had the company been informed concerning the real character of the occupancy.

Factories more than any other class of risks except dwellings, have occasioned disputes as to what constitutes occupancy. During seasons of dull times, strikes, or on account of financial embarrassments, active work is likely to be suspended for a longer or shorter time. Often such suspensions are of a character that amounts to at least a temporary abandonment of the care and oversight of the premises, producing, so far as the underwriter is concerned, all the evils of a permanent abandonment. Hence, stipulations are frequently incorporated in the policy, involving forfeiture if it ceases to be operated for more than a specified number of days, and in such case, of course, a violation will incur the penalty. But when no such express limitation is made, if the temporary non-use of premises is such as might be regarded as a natural incident of the business, the courts are apt to regard it with leniency. Thus in Whitney vs. Ins. Co. (7 Ins. Law Jour., 477) through. the breaking of machinery and other causes work in a saw-mill had been interrupted at intervals for several months, and no work had been done for sixteen days before the fire, but the lumber was on hand to continue the business, and it was held to be no vacancy. The court said : "Occupation of a dwelling-house is living in it. But people do not live in a saw-mill. In Keith vs. Ins. Co. (10 Allen, 531) the plaintiff closed up a trip-hammer shop, and it was held to be vacant. A shop of that kind ordinarily has people working in it on every working day. A saw-mill is different. If a custom mill, it must depend on the logs brought to it for business. In any case when driven by water-power it must rely on the supply of water, and must be idle when that fails." In the case of Keith referred to, the shop had not been actively used for more than thirty days, but the tools were all there and it was visited every day to see that all was right. Yet this was not occupancy. Again, in American Ins. Co. vs. Foster (9 Ins. Law Jour., 268), property insured as a school-house was afterwards abandoned for that purpose and used as a dwelling, and it was held that the utmost which could be claimed under the policy was a brief temporary vacancy, such as is usual in school-houses. Neither as a dwelling nor school could a vacancy of several months be allowed.

It will thus be seen that in case of those risks which are used only for business or manufacturing purposes, the safe rule requires that any prolonged non-use, which is not an ordinary incident of the hazard, should be treated as a vacancy for which consent must be obtained. The ordinary stipulation regarding occupancy has been held to refer simply to insurances on a building, but where personal property only is the subject, it is obvious that vacancy may sometimes be equally important. Therefore, in such case, it is safer to stipulate against the premises containing the insured property becoming vacant.

Carr vs. Ins. Cos., 13 Ins. Law Jour., 443.

PROHIBITED RISKS.

All policies expressly prohibit the keeping or storing on the premises of certain articles which experience has shown to be incendiary in their character, like gunpowder and explosive oils, and a violation will forfeit the insurance. But it frequently happens that the nature of the risk, or the ordinary method of using the property, is such as to involve to some extent the presence of the prohibited article. The sale of coal-oils and gunpowder is often a part of the regular business of a store-keeper, the use of naphtha or benzine may be an essential part of a business, or the keeping of a limited amount of kerosene necessary for lighting the dwelling. Hence, numerous disputes have arisen as to how the prohibition must be interpreted in those cases where the written description of the risk itself might seem to imply a consent to keep the forbidden article; hence, too, the importance of particular inquiries by the agent in all cases where there is reason to suppose that a prohibited article may be innocently used or kep

The mere presence in minute quantities of a forbidden article is not necessarily a violation. The amount must be sufficient to violate the spirit of the prohibition. Just what is such an amount is a difficult question to determine. In Wheeler vs. Ins. Co. (8 Ins. Law Jour., 318) it was held, that keeping a burning-fluid in the limited quantity needed for filling lamps was not a violation, where its use for light was not expressly prohibited. In Mears vs. Ins. Co. (9 Ins. Law Jour., 139) the bringing of a small quantity of benzine on the premises on a single occasion for cleaning machinery was not a violation. In Bayly vs. Ins. Co. (4 Ins. Law Jour., 503) a small quantity of saltpetre kept to cure meat in a store was held not to be sufficient in amount to be a substantial violation. In Winans vs. Ins. Co. (5 Ins. Law Jour., 203) and in Bennett vs. Ins. Co. (9 Ins. Law Jour., 585) the knowledge of the agent that coal-oils were used for lighting excused the violation. On the other hand, in Matson vs. Ins. Co. the use of kerosene for lighting where expressly prohibited, and in Wheeler vs. Ins. Co. (12 Ins. Law Jour., 834) a barrel of naphtha brought to a mill for destroying moths, were both held to be violations. It will thus be seen that the presence of a prohibited article, even in limited quantities, is liable to be a ground of dispute and may result in forfeiture. If known by the agent, he should charge a rate commensurate with the hazard and give consent for its use, or he should decline the risk, as the case might be.

It frequently happens that inflammables of the same general character and equally dangerous are used, but which are somewhat different in their composition from those forbidden, or they are kept on the premises a short distance away. Thus in Sperry vs. Ins. Co. (15 Ins. Law Jour., 270) dynamite was kept, this was held to be a violation of the provision against nitro-glycerine. On the other hand, in Mosely vs. Ins. Co. (13 Ins. Law Jour., 97) it was left to a jury to say whether turpentine was an explosive, and in Willis vs. Ins. Co. (8 Ins. Law Jour., 449) whether alcohol was an explosive. In Carlin vs. Ins. Co. (12 Ins. Law Jour., 388) the petroleum was kept in an adjoining engine-room, and therefore was held not to be on the premises. In Hicks vs. Ins. Co. (8 Ins. Law Jour., 320) it was left for a jury to say whether mineral sperm-oil was included in a provision against kerosene. In all these cases the spirit of the prohibition was violated, if not the letter.

See also Bennett vs. Ins. Co., 9 Ins. Law Jour., 585 ; Mears vs. Ins. Co., 8 Ins. Law Jour., 139.

But the cases most frequently before the courts and requiring the most careful inquiry by the agent, are those where a prohibited article is kept as a part of a regular stock-in-trade. Country store-keepers are especially apt to deal in dangerous combustibles and explosives. Sometimes the language of the policy is so explicit that a forfeiture is the result, but in many cases the description of the property as " his stock as a country store-keeper," has been held to amount to a tacit consent to keep such articles. In Wheeler vs. Ins. Co. (15 Ins. Law Jour., 184), it was held that insurance on a woolen-mill implies a knowledge that naphtha was necessarily used in the business. In Collins vs. Ins. Co. (8 Ins. Law Jour., 453) the presence of saltpetre was excused because it was an article usually kept in drug-stores. But in Portsmouth Ins. Co. vs. Brinckley (2 Ins. Law Jour., 842),in Whitmarsh vs. Ins. Co. (2 Allen, 581), and in Steinbach vs. Ins. Co. (13 Wal., 183) the courts refused to recognize this doctrine, and insisted that a distinct, printed prohibition could not be overcome by insuring in general terms a line of goods which might by custom contain the forbidden article. The last-named case was in the United States Supreme Court, and it was there held that an insurance on fire-crackers and "other articles in his line of business" would not cover a forbidden article even so closely allied as fire-works.

In all cases, therefore, where prohibited articles are included among the subjects of insurance, special consent should be obtained and paid for, or the insured should be notified that their presence is likely to forfeit the insurance. The use of gas-machines within or too near premises, contrary to provisions in the policy, has been a frequent source of litigation, and should be carefully looked after.

Winans vs. Ins. Co., 5 Ins. Law Jour., 203 ; Arkell vs. Ins. Co., 6 Ins. Law Jour., 251; N. W. Mut. Life Ins. Co. vs. Ins. Co., 40 Wis., 446.

ALTERATIONS AND REPAIRS.

Trifling repairs from time to time are essential to the preservation of the property, they are incidental to the risk, and the courts regard the insured as entitled to make them without the company's consent, so long as they are only such ordinary repairs as are needed to every building. Tinners may repair a leaky roof, plumbers may stop leaks or remove obstructions in pipes, and painters may renew the paint, though the tools employed by each slightly increase the hazard for the time being.

Townsend vs. Ins. Co., 18 N. Y., 168; Ottawa Co. vs. Ins. Co., 28 U.C. Q. B., 518; Dorn vs. Ins. Co., 5 Ins. Law Jour., 183; James vs. Ins. Co., 4 Ins. Law Jour., 9; O'Neil vs. Ins. Co., 3 N. Y., 122.

But it is important to note that such repairing must be restricted to that which is ordinary and of no great magnitude. The moment these operations become extensive in their character, even though they are necessary, the insurer has a right to object on account of the increase of risk which the policy prohibits. Even in the absence of a distinct prohibition against repairs, if it can be shown that the risk was materially increased thereby, forfeiture may result, especially if a loss can be traced to this cause, and the repairs were extensive in their character.

Curry vs. Ins. Co., 10 Pick., 535.

All substantial alterations of a building are looked on by the companies as an increase of risk. Where, as so often happens, such alterations effect an increase in the size of the original structure, insurers properly regard the risk as one which was not contemplated in the contract, and a loss-claim is likely to be resisted whether resulting from this cause or not. Thus in Lyman vs. Ins. Co. (14 Allen, 329) it was held that a deliberate, considerable alteration not incidental to the ordinary use of the building, and prolonged for three weeks, increasing the risk at the time of the fire, although not permanently, nor causing the fire, avoids the policy. The policy itself usually stipulates against material alterations or repairs, or restricts them to such as can be done within a limited time, and any excess of this limit will work a forfeiture.

To avoid controversy, therefore, consent should be obtained for all material alterations or repairs beyond such as are expressly permitted by the contract.

INCREASE OF RISK GENERALLY.

There are many other ways besides those heretofore referred to in which a risk may be increased in violation of the policy. Any important modification whatever of the hazard which makes it essentially different in character from that which was originally assumed and which materially increases the danger from fire, should be looked on as an increase of risk. The courts ask two prominent questions on this subject—has the risk been modified or altered in a way not contemplated in the original contract, and is the alteration one which, if known, would have been likely to call for an increased premium or to have induced a cancellation? Whatever changes suggest an affirmative answer to these questions, whether in the manner of use or occupancy, in the arrangements or character of the subject, or in its surroundings, should be treated as an increase of risk about which the insurer is entitled to information. In Daniels vs. Ins. Co. (12 Ins. Law Jour., 379) the court pronounced the presence of a stove in a finishing-room, where there was frequently a large quantity of inflammable naphtha-gas, a manifest increase of risk. So, in Osterloh vs. Ins. Co. (13 Ins. Law Jour., 475), a pipe had been thrust through the ceiling and roof in contravention of the policy requirements, which would have resulted in forfeiture had it not been waived by the company. In Cole vs. Ins. Co. (14 Ins. Law Jour., 453) the court declared that the erection of a wooden drying-house one story high, fourteen feet from a brick planing-mill, and heated by steam from a boiler in the main building, was a self-evident increase of risk. In Long vs. Beeber (14 Ins. Law Jour., 622) a steam-thresher was temporarily located in an adjacent barn, and it was held that, even though done by a tenant without the knowledge of insured, if the risk was increased the policy was avoided. The court used the following language: "The company for a fixed price insured the building as it was at the date of the policy. It took upon itself that hazard and none other ; and to avoid all dispute as to what it did insure, the condition was introduced that if the risk was increased by the erection or occupation of neighboring buildings, or by any means whatever, without the assent of the company, the policy should be void, and subject to this condition the plaintiff accepted this policy. There is no doubt whatever about the binding character of this contract, and if the insured did in fact, without the assent of the insurer, either by himself or tenant, do anything to increase the risk, the contract was violated, and he must suffer the consequences." The principle here laid down should govern the agent in judging whether there has been an increase of risk. In Francis vs. Ins. Co. (25 N. J., 78) a somewhat similar provision was violated by erecting a small addition to the insured store in which was placed a quantity of hay for a cow. The hay took fire, and the court declared as a matter of law that the policy was forfeited.

Another important phase of this question was well illustrated in the case of Washington Ins. Co vs. Davison, 30 Md., 91. The insurance was on a sulphuric-acid factory; in point of fact, nitric as well as sulphuric acid was manufactured. The premises had been inspected by the agent, and the court declared that in writing such a risk the insurer should have known that the manufacture of nitric acid was necessary as a part of the process. The incapacity of the inspector would form no defense. In other words, whatever obvious features of the business are likely to involve an increase of risk beyond that which is apparently assumed in the mere description, should be noted by the agent.

CONCURRENCY IN POLICY-WRITING.

The greatest difficulty encountered by the companies in adjusting loss-claims, aside from agreeing with the claimant as to the actual amount of damages, has arisen through non-concurrency, as it is termed, of the various policies covering the property. One policy sometimes contains stipulations, such as co-insurance, or three-quarter loss or value clauses, limiting the liability, which are absent from another. Frequently one policy covers one or more items not included in the other, without specifically limiting its liability on each ; or one may be a floating policy, as in the case of railroad insurance, while another may insure a specific sum on the property destroyed. One may cover only a single interest, and another include several interests. One may be liable for any actual damages, and another only for damages in excess of a certain amount.

In all such cases the great difficulty is to determine as between the companies what proportion of the loss each one should bear. All policies now contain the contribution-clause, which restricts each company to its pro-rata share of the loss, and various rules have been adopted by underwriters and laid down by the courts for determining in such cases how the pro-rata is to be computed. But the companies are far from being harmonious as to what rules are correct ; while the courts have generally contented themselves with framing a doctrine which shall seem most equitable in the particular case before them, regardless of its want of equity under other conditions. In fact, neither law nor mathematics furnishes any precise general rules of equitable apportionment which are applicable to all cases of non-concurrency. But the courts do insist that the insured shall recover the largest amount to which he would be entitled under any fair construction of the contracts, regardless of any want of equity in its apportionment among the companies.

Royal Ins. Co. vs. Roedel, 4 Ins. Law Jour., 840 ; Robbins vs. Ins. Co., Hine & Nichols' Dig., 170 ; Angelrodt vs. Ins. Co., 31 Mo., 593 ; Haley vs. Ins. Co., 12 Gray, 349 ; Blake vs. Ins. Co., 12 Gray, 265 ; Bardwell vs. Ins. Co., 6 Ins. Law Jour., 413.

The consequence is that where the policies are non-concurrent, not only are the companies liable to be involved in disputes among themselves, but those whose contracts, owing to the absence of limitations, can be construed to afford the largest indemnity, are likely to be saddled with the largest proportion of the loss. In Sherman vs. Ins. Co., cited above, one company insured on live-stock simply, while another limited its liability on any one animal to a specific sum; the consequence was that, though both policies were for nearly the same amount, the second company escaped with less than half the liability of the first. In Carlwitz vs. Ins. Co. (12 Ins. Law Jour., 127) the policy was written for specific amounts on various items, on some of which the loss was heavy and on others none ; and the court instructed that the claimant could only look in such a case for indemnity to the particular fund intended to indemnify the property; an excess of loss on one item could not be made good·from the surplus on another, thus showing the great advantage to the company of specific insurances. In Angelrodt vs. Ins. Co., *supra*, one policy included other interests besides those covered by the first policy ; a lower court had made an apportionment of the loss between the two, which the appellate court declared to be correct, if it had fully indemnified the insured ; but failing in this another rule must be adopted which would furnish the indemnity. The addition of another interest to the second policy compelled a larger contribution from the first, notwithstanding it was specific.

These cases, to which others might be added, show the importance, first, of making the policy-writing as specific both in regard to the property and interests as the circumstances will allow; second, of insisting that where a certain amount of other insurance is a condition, such other insurance shall be likewise specific ; third, of having other insurance concurrent both as to the interests and property covered and as to limitations of any kind on the liabilities. The company that insures, for instance, without a co-insurance clause is at a disadvantage, if this clause exists in other insurance on the same property. Not only, therefore, should the agent carefully inquire regarding the amount of other insurance on the property, but with regard to its apportionment and limitations, and, if authorized to contract, should seek to so frame his own policy that his company will not suffer through non-concurrency.

Printed forms, if properly constructed, are desirable so far as resulting concurrency is concerned. Printed forms, however, are liable to be gotten up too much in the interest of the insured, but whether printed or written, all the policies on the same risk should read alike.

Indorsements and Modifications by the Agent.

Agents who are authorized to contract are usually permitted by law to consent to such subsequent minor modifications of the contract as they might have made in the first instance where the instrument itself does not forbid their doing so, and where the modifications might reasonably be supposed to be within the scope of their powers.

Pitney vs. Ins. Co., 4 Ins. Law Jour., 765; Pechner vs. Ins. Co., 4 Ins. Law Jour., 782, and cases there cited.

But this power is never intended to be applied to the printed portion of the policy, which frequently contains stipulations forbidding it; and in those States which have standard-policy laws, such a tampering with the printed portion would be, as stated elsewhere, a penal offense against the statute. Particularly should an agent avoid the dangerous assumption of verbal agreements to modify the policy; whatever changes in or additions to the written portion may be asked for should be carefully considered, reduced to writing, indorsed on the policy, and reported to the company. It is a sound legal principle that verbal evidence cannot be admitted to alter the terms of a written instrument, and in case of dispute it is only by a legal subterfuge that the proof of a mere verbal agreement to modify can be accepted. A written contract should contain within itself all the stipulations between the parties.

Mercantile Ins. Co. vs. Jaynes, 7 Ins. Law Jour., 754; Hearne vs. Ins. Co., 4 Ins. Law Jour., 582; Aurora Ins. Co. vs. Eddy, 55 Ill., 213.

The company is entitled to know at all times the conditions attached to its contracts, and the precise character of the risks it is assuming. By just so much as the original policy is modified by subsequent consent of the agent, the company is likely to be uninformed on these points. Such modifications, too, are almost invariably in the interest of the insured and usually contemplate an increase of risk without any increase of premium. It is as much the legal duty of the agent therefore to notify the company of any modifications as of the terms of the original contract. Waivers and modifications by the agent which were unauthorized by or unknown to the companies have entailed more losses on the latter than almost any other one cause outside of the fires themselves.

Where the policy expressly limits the agent's powers in this respect, or requires all modifications of the contract to be indorsed in writing, a violation by the agent, besides rendering him legally liable for the consequences, will generally prove ineffectual to accomplish the object sought. Where the agent's power is thus limited, the insured is bound to take notice of the fact at his own peril. In Walsh vs. Ins. Co. (7 Ins. Law

Jour., 423) the policy required consent to be indorsed in writing, and the agent, who had power to contract, verbally consented to a vacancy, of which he made a memorandum, but made no indorsement as required on the policy. The court said : "The plaintiff is presumed to have known what the contract contained, and the proof tends to the conclusion that this provision was brought to his notice. He saw fit, however, to accept the assurance of the agent that an entry in the register was sufficient. It is difficult to see how, upon the law of contracts and agency, the plaintiff can recover. The entry in the register was not an indorsement on the policy. The oral consent was an act in excess of the known authority of the agent. The provision was designed to protect the company against collusion and fraud, and the dangers and uncertainty of oral testimony."

See, also, Crescent Ins. Co. vs. Griffin, 14 Ins. Law Jour., 278; Enos vs. Ins. Co., 15 Ins. Law Jour., 138.

Again, it is only the agent who is authorized to issue the policy in the first place that can consent as a rule to its modification, whether by indorsement or otherwise. A solicitor or agent whose power is limited to receiving applications can sometimes render the company responsible for information furnished to him at the time of receiving the application regarding vacancy, other insurance, alterations, and the like, because he is then the medium of communication between the applicant and the company. But when once the contract has been completed, his relations to it are at an end. As he had no power to make it so, he has no right to consent to its alteration.

Wilson vs. Ins. Co., 4 Kern., 418; Sykes vs. Ins. Co., 34 Penn. St., 79; Robinson vs. Ins. Co., 3 Dutch., 134; N. E. Ins. Co. vs. Schettler, 38 Ill., 166; Strickland vs. Ins. Co., 14 Ins. Law Jour., 868.

In one respect, however, the relations of the soliciting agent are not always ended. Where notice is required to be given for the mere purpose of information to the company, where no acquiescence by the latter is needed and no party is specified to whom it must be given, as in the case of notice of loss, it has sometimes been held that notice to an agent procuring the insurance is sufficient, that the medium through whom the insurance was procured may be further relied on to convey additional information. But this doctrine only applies to those cases where the insured might reasonably assume that such notice was sufficient.

Hartford Ins. Co. vs. Smith, 7 Ins. Law Jour., 140; Union Ins. Co. vs. Wilkinson, 13 Wall., 222; Schenck vs. Ins. Co., 4 Zab., 447.

In general, therefore, a soliciting agent should regard himself as without any authority to act in respect to any matters pertaining to a completed contract, and should so state to the insured whenever asked to make changes, or whenever questioned in regard to his authority to make changes, but for greater safety should communicate to the company all information he may receive regarding it. Especially should he be on his guard against seeming by his conduct towards the insured to assume any responsibility in relation to the contract. Even though a soliciting agent should be regarded as a proper party to receive a notice of loss, which usually he is not, he would have no right to accept notice of a vacancy, increase of risk, change of title, incumbrance, or any of those matters which affect the character of the contract, and which might influence the company to cancel or increase the rate. In short, the solicitor, outside of the special work for which he is employed, has properly no relations with the company beyond the ordinary duty of an employé to communicate to his employer such facts as the latter ought to know.

Harrison vs.Ins. Co., 9 Allen, 231; Miner vs. Ins. Co., 29 Wis., 693; Phœnix Ins. Co. vs. Lawrence, 4 Met., 9.

Again, it does not necessarily follow that because an agent is authorized to issue policies, he is therefore authorized to make any subsequent modifications of any kind in their conditions. As was said in Sohnes vs. Ins. Co. (121 Mass., 438), something more than a special agency must be shown to justify such a conclusion on the part of the insured. Authority, or apparent authority, to thus act as a general agent must be established. A person deals with the agent in matters in excess of his apparent special authority at his peril. The printed conditions of a policy constitute the general form under which the company elects to issue its contracts. Blanks are left in this form, presumably to be filled up at his discretion by an authorized representative. These facts may be regarded as in a measure a notice both to the agent and the insured that the former has usually no right to mutilate or nullify, or introduce anything inconsistent with the printed conditions ; that in those respects, at least, even the powers of an agent authorized to contract are limited. He has no right to contract in a way inconsistent with the policy-blank. Thus, in Reynolds vs. Ins. Co. (36 Mich., 181), an attempt was made to show an oral contract for insurance with the agent on a risk belonging to a class that the agent was not allowed to insure ; but the court held that even proof of the fact that the agent solicited the risk and received the premium was not proof of his power to bind the company in the face of his commission and the policy to the contrary. As was said by the court, the fact that he was local agent could only imply authority to insure in the mode allowed by the charter, and to take such risks as the policies in common use by the agents would warrant. In Barry vs. Ins.

Co. (15 Ins. Law Jour., 789) an agent, who had no authority to insure hulls, undertook to insure a yacht by filling in a cargo-blank whose printed language was wholly inappropriate, and it was held that the inconsistency was sufficient notice to the insured that the agent was exceeding his authority. To this class also belong those numerous cases where it has been held that the agent, unless vested with special authority for that purpose, has no right to waive requirements regarding proofs of loss.

Sohnes vs. Ins. Co., 6 Ins. Law Jour., 472, and cases there cited.

The safe rule for the agent is to limit all indorsements to those matters where he is explicitly authorized by the company thus to modify, and, above all, to avoid such as shall essentially alter the character of the contract, the risk, or the parties. Where, as in Massachusetts and New York, a standard policy-form is prescribed, any modification of the language whatever beyond that which the law permits would be a penal offense against statutory law.

CANCELLATION.

When the agent has been instructed to cancel a risk, he is legally bound to carry out the instruction without any unnecessary delay. The penalty to which he is exposed in case of negligence was illustrated in the recent case of Phœnix Ins. Co. vs. Pratt, in the 16th Ins. Law Jour., already cited, where the agent assumed the responsibility of delaying until he could communicate further with the company. The risk burned before an answer could be received, and he was held personally liable to the company for the loss.

Two things are essential to a complete cancellation; notification to the insured or some party authorized to represent him, and a tender at the same time of the unearned premium.

Continental Ins. Co. vs. Bunsby, 15 Ins. Law Jour., 736; Griffey vs. Ins. Co., 15 Ins. Law Jour., 198; Ætna Ins. Co. vs. Weisinger, 14 Ins. Law Jour., 151; Ætna Ins. Co. vs. Maguire, 51 Ill., 342.

The notice should be given and the tender made to the insured himself if possible, or if not, then to some party authorized to act for him in the matter, and the policy should be taken up and returned to the company. It by no means follows that the party who was authorized by the insured to procure the insurance, is also authorized to accept a notice of cancellation. This has often proved a fatal mistake on the part of the agent. The true doctrine was laid down in Rothschild vs. Ins. Co. (7 Ins. Law Jour., 639), where it was held that an agency to procure insurance is ended when the insurance is procured and the policy delivered to the principal ; that the agent to procure the insurance (*i. e.*, the broker) has no power after the delivery of the policy to his principal to consent to a cancellation. In Von Wein vs. Ins. Co. (15 Ins. Law Jour., 158), although the policy contained a stipulation that the party procuring the policy should be deemed the agent of the insured in matters relating to the insurance, it was held that a broker employed by the insured to procure the policy was not on that account to be deemed his agent to receive notice of cancellation ; that the cancellation did not relate to the insurance. A broker or intermediary can only be safely dealt with where it can be satisfactorily shown that the entire care of managing and looking after his insurances has been placed in his hands by the insured. Thus in Gatti vs. Ins. Co. (9 Ins. Law Jour., 158) it appeared that the party who procured the policy and paid the premium was allowed entire control of the property, collecting and using the rents in his own way, and it was held that authority to cancel, as well as to insure, was within the apparent scope of his power.

Notice of an intention to cancel is not sufficient. It must be a notice of actual cancellation, coupled with a tender of the return premium, and the amount of the unearned premium must be tendered in cash ; but, if no cash is due, simple notice is sufficient. Where a note has been given this should be returned, unless some payment on it is due or owing, in which case the tender should still be cash.

Bergesson vs. Ins. Co., 38 Cal., 541; Bunsby vs. Ins. Co., *supra;* Griffey vs. Ins. Co., *supra;* Hawthorn vs. Ins. Co., 55 Barb., 28; Ætna Ins. Co. vs. Webster, 6 Wall., 129; Emmott vs. Ins. Co., 7 R. I., 562; Southside Ins. Co. vs. Muller, 8 Ins. Law Jour., 260; Home Ins. Co. vs. Curtis, 5 Ins. Law Jour., 120.

The risk should also be canceled on the agent's register, and the return of the policy demanded and secured, if possible, but the actual return of the policy is not essential to a cancellation. It is the duty of the insured to return it, but his refusal to do so or to accept the tender will not keep the contract in force. Where cancellation is demanded by the insured, however, he is usually bound to tender the policy in order to make it effectual, if in his possession.

Grace vs. Ins. Co., 8 Ins. Law Jour., 95; Amer. Ins. Co. vs. Woodruff, 34 Mich., 6.

In Grace vs. Ins. Co., just cited, the attempt of the agent to cancel was defeated by his simply notifying the insured that upon the return of the policy he would cancel it and refund the premium. He should have tendered the premium and demanded a return of the policy. The insured, however, may waive the immediate repayment of the premium if he chooses, but the understanding should be clear that the contract is regarded as ended by both parties. Cancellation can only be enforced by either party by virtue of the policy-stipulation to that effect, and the courts insist that it can be exercised only in strict compliance with the condition.

Ætna Ins. Co. vs. Weisinger, 14 Ins. Law Jour., 86, and cases there cited.

A mere solicitor has no right to cancel of his own motion ; the agent must be one authorized to contract. In Jacobs vs. Ins. Co. (14 Ins. Law Jour., 633) it was declared that a power to receive applications, premium-notes, and cash premiums does not include a power to cancel policies. Nor is the offer to prove such cancellation helped by showing that the policy was sent by the agent to the company as a surrendered policy, unless the company accepted it as such. But a solicitor or any other party may, of course, cancel, if authorized to do so. The most important point to be borne in mind in all cases is that no cancellation will be regarded as effectual by the court until whatever may be due as unearned premium has been actually paid or tendered, or its payment distinctly waived by the insured himself or a party fully authorized to represent him.

The natural disposition of an agent to regard the insured as a client, whose interest he must protect by securing other insurance before canceling, has sometimes caused litigation. The agent's first duty is to himself and his company, and he has no right to make the execution of an order to cancel contingent upon his ability to place the risk elsewhere, thereby rendering himself liable in case the risk should burn while he is neglecting the instructions of his company.

Ætna Ins. Co. vs. Maguire, 51 Ill., 342; Goit vs. Ins. Co., 25 Barb., 189; Train vs. Ins. Co., 5 Ins. Law Jour., 177. See, also, Phœnix Ins. Co. vs. Pratt, already cited.

The mere possession of the policy by another will not justify the conclusion that he is authorized to surrender it for cancellation. In Bennett vs. Ins. Co. (115 Mass., 241) the surrender for cancellation of a policy by the assignee who held it as security, without the knowledge of the insured, was declared invalid.

RENEWALS.

Renewals have not unfrequently proved pitfalls for unwary agents. The general doctrine is that a renewal is simply an extension of the original contract. The effect is the same as if the date and duration of the original policy were altered to correspond with those of the renewal-receipt. All the conditions and stipulations remain as at first. A violation of any will have the same effect as before the renewal took place.

Aurora Ins. Co. vs. Kranich, 6 Ins. Law Jour., 676 ; Sheppard vs. Ins. Co., 12 Ins. Law Jour., 817, and cases there cited.

But this is true only so far as the renewal contemplates no change in the original contract, or the conditions, so far as known to the insurer or agent, continue the same. A change in the law, such as the passage of a valued-policy act, will be imported into a subsequent renewal.

Brady vs. Ins. Co., 11 Mich., 425.

A change in the apparent distribution of the risk, as where the original policy was on specific items, while the renewals insured only a gross sum, will convert the latter into a general insurance.

Driggs vs. Ins. Co., 10 Barb., 440.

Any changes contemplated in the original contract should be expressed in the renewal-receipt, and unless such changes are contemplated, care should be taken that the matter should not be left in doubt through the use of ambiguous language. In Sheppard vs. Ins. Co. (12 Ins. Law Jour., 817) the agent gave a renewal-receipt some weeks after the termination of the policy, bearing also such later date and continuing a year, and a suit was required to determine its legal effect. A hasty promise to renew may be unwise. Such promise, if an actual, completed agreement, amounts to an oral contract of insurance. In King vs. Ins. Co. (13 Ins. Law Jour., 146) it was claimed that the agent had thus promised to renew, and the court held, that if the evidence showed not merely preliminary negotiations, but a verbal contract complete in all its terms, it was binding, and non-payment of premium would not defeat the insurance until demand had been made for it, or the insured had been notified of the company's refusal to carry the risk. Entries made by the agent in his register were not admitted as evidence to the contrary.

See, also, Roger Williams Ins. Co. vs. Carrington, 9 Ins. Law Jour., 577.

But in O'Reilly vs. Corporation (15 Ins. Law Jour., 83) a mere casual conversation with the agent requesting renewal at a subsequent date, which contemplated further action and where no premium was paid, was not recognized as a valid renewal where the policy stipulated that it should not be liable unless the premium for the renewal was paid. The agent should, therefore, confine himself to a distinct understanding that the policy can only be renewed upon the payment of premium and delivery of the renewal-receipt. After an agreement to renew has once been made, no change whatever in the conditions of the original policy can been made without the consent of the insured. In Hay vs. Ins. Co. (8 Ins. Law Jour., 633) a second policy was issued in compliance with such an agreement, which, unknown to the insured, contained conditions not in the first, and the court held that it must be reformed to correspond with the first. The only proper course for the company would have been to have notified the insured that it declined to continue under the original contract, but would make a new one if desired. All modifications made by a renewal, therefore, should be distinctly brought to the notice of the insured.

WHAT TO DO IN CASE OF LOSS.

Any discussion of the delicate and complicated legal questions involved in the adjustment of losses is foreign to the plan of this book. The work of the adjuster is usually intrusted by the companies to experts in this branch. Familiarity with the subject by the ordinary agent is rather discouraged than otherwise, from the danger that the agent may be tempted to act on a limited and partial knowledge, and thus embarrass rather than facilitate a satisfactory settlement. Almost the only things which the ordinary agent requires to know relating to adjustments are what not to do. But he frequently has other and important duties to perform in the interest of his company in case of loss. The first of these, after notifying the company, is to care for the proper preservation of the damaged property. The doctrine of abandonment, so familiar in marine insurance, is not recognized in fire insurance. The owner cannot compel the company to accept his damaged property and pay him its full original value ; he retains his title after the loss as before it. But in practice the companies sometimes agree to take the damaged stock and are entitled to do so upon payment of a constructive total loss. Whether they do or not, the agent, as the representative of their interests, is entitled to take such steps as the owner may permit for the further protection of the property. But in doing so the fact should be borne in mind, that the damaged goods remain the property of the insured after the fire as before it. It is at his risk, must be cared for at his expense, and he has no right to claim against the insurer for any additional loss or damage chargeable to his own negligence. The insured is bound to do all in his power to save his property, and to care for the salvage.

Arnold on Mar. Ins., 875 ; Marshall on Mar. Ins., 497 ; Wood on Ins., 776.

This does not mean, however, that he must seek to restore it to its condition before the fire, but simply to protect it against theft and further deterioration. He is not bound to have shirts and collars relaundried, that were damaged by water.

Hoffman vs. Ins. Co., 32 N. Y., 405.

The agent, therefore, should be on his guard against relieving the insured of these responsibilities. His aim should rather be to see that they are assumed and properly acted on; for, unless the insured can be shown to have been guilty of culpable negligence; usually a difficult thing to do; the loss through subsequent deterioration is likely to fall on the company. Another duty devolving upon the agent is to quietly acquire such information regarding the circumstances attending the loss as will aid in discovering the cause, and whether any fraud has been attempted; that class of facts, in short, which can best be secured by one who is on the spot at the time and is familiar with the surroundings.

Naturally, the first move on the part of the insured will usually be to consult the local agent about the recovery of his damages and the steps to be taken, and here begins the chief danger to the company. As a rule the agent should never seek the insured for this purpose. His duty is simply to promptly notify the company of all the facts in his possession. The contract requires the insured to seek the company, and give it the stipulated notice with due diligence. When a particular method or party is designated in the policy, the notice should conform to the requirement. Otherwise the general rule is that a verbal notice to the local agent is sufficient. It may be given either by the insured or some party authorized to represent him, and must be sufficient to apprise the company of the loss, and give an opportunity for examination. It must be given as soon as possible.

Platte vs. Ass'n, 6 Ins. Law Jour., 595 ; Hartford Ins. Co. vs. Smith, 7 Ins. Law Jour., 401 ; People's Ins. Co. vs. Spencer, 53 Penn. St., 353 ; Sleeper vs. Ins. Co., 5 Ins. Law Jour., 537 ; Riggs vs. Ins. Co., 20 N. H., 198 ; O'Brien vs. Ins. Co., 8 Ins. Law Jour., 517.

The agent, therefore, if consulted by the insured, should direct him to conform to the policy-requirements, and should inform him that the company alone has authority in the premises. If the policy requires a written notice, he should insist that it be given in this form by the insured, and then immediately forward it to the company. If the stipulation is that it be given to a particular party, as the secretary, he should direct the insured to so send it. By failing to observe these rules, the agent has repeatedly waived a proper compliance with the requirement of the policy.

Brink vs. Ins. Co., 6 Ins. Law Jour., 707 ; Bennett vs. Ins. Co., 6 Ins. Law Jour., 189 ; Home Ins. Co. vs. Ins. Co., 6 Ins. Law Jour., 739.

Above all, the agent should strictly refrain from expressing any opinion regarding the company's liability. The hasty denial of liability, or conduct which justified the insured in believing that it would be useless to attempt a compliance with the policy-requirement as to notice and proofs, has time and again justified him before the courts in failing to do either.

Lycoming Ins. Co. vs. Dunmore, 5 Ins. Law Jour., 93 ; Aurora Ins. Co. vs. Kranich, 6 Ins. Law Jour., 676 ; Findeisen vs. Ins. Co., 15 Ins. Law Jour., 90; Karibo vs. Ins. Co., 15 Ins. Law Jour., 478 ; Akin vs. Ins. Co., 6 Ins. Law Jour., 341.

Substantially the same remarks apply to proofs as to notice of loss when the blanks have been forwarded to the agent, except that the proofs, being intended as evidence to the company of the exact nature and extent of its liabilities, should always be in writing, deliberately prepared, and with a strict observance of every requirement.

Columbian Ins. Co. vs. Rogers, 2 Pet., 52 ; Savage vs. Ins. Co., 52 N. Y., 502 ; Bumstead vs. Ins. Co., 12 N. Y., 81 ; Jennings vs. Ins. Co., 2 Den., 75 ; Hartford Ins. Co. vs. Smith, 7 Ins. Law Jour., 108.

Proofs should always be made by the insured, if possible, or his authorized representative. In his absence they may be made by a party naturally authorized to represent him, or in such a case they may be made by the party in interest to whom the loss is payable.

Kernochen vs. Ins. Co., 17 N. Y., 428 ; Pratt vs. Ins. Co., 55 N. Y., 505 ; Ayers vs. Ins. Co., 17 Iowa, 176.

As in the case of the application, they should be filled by the insured, if possible, but he is entitled to such information as is necessary to make them satisfactory and complete in their form. It is the duty of the insurer to point out defects which he desires to have remedied.

Blake vs. Ins. Co., 12 Gray, 265 ; Clarke vs. Ins. Co., 6 Cush., 324 ; Young vs. Ins. Co., 6 Ins. Law Jour., 549 ; Mason vs. Ins. Co., 6 Ins. Law Jour., 842.

In fine, the chief duty of the agent after the loss may be summed up as that of aiding the insured in complying with all the requirements of his contract, and avoiding everything which may give him ground for claiming that such compliance has been excused. The whole question of subsequent liability belongs to the company and its adjuster. The agent is under no obligation to discuss it, and should refer the insured to them for any information on the subject. If by accident the policy is lost or burned, the insured is not prejudiced in his rights thereby. He is entitled to such facts in relation to it in making out his proofs as the agent may possess.

MUTUAL INSURANCE.

In what has been said heretofore, special reference has been had to the law governing in the case of ordinary stock companies, but the same principles control in the case of mutual companies, except as they may be modified by the peculiarities of the latter form of insurance. In some important respects, however, the legal relations of the parties in mutual and in stock companies are essentially different, and these differences impose their modifications on the law in the two cases. In the stock company the corporate members or proprietors and the insured are two distinct classes, sustaining, in a mercantile sense, antagonistic relations to each other. In the mutual company, on the contrary, they constitute a single class; the insured are also by virtue of that relation the stockholders. The consequence of this distinction is that the insured member in a mutual company is assumed to be possessed of a knowledge of its corporate powers and business rules and methods, and to be vested with a responsibility for his own acts which are not attributable to an ordinary policy-holder. In the language of the court in Krug vs. Ins. Co. (5 Ins. Law Jour., 7), persons insuring in mutual companies are associated in the nature of limited or special partners, and they sustain towards the companies in many respects the relations of partners rather than those of customers. In a word, the member is ordinarily bound by the charter and by-laws of the company, whether he has any actual knowledge of them or not.

Fuller vs. Ins. Co., 4 Ins. Law Jour., 841, and cases there cited ; Hackney vs. Ins. Co., 4 Barr., 185 ; Hope Ins. Co. vs. Beekman, 47 Mo., 93.

The charter and by-laws of the company enter by implication into all its contracts, whether they are expressed in the policy or not. The insured is not usually allowed to plead ignorance concerning them, nor to claim that he was misled in regard to them. Whatever is done by the officers within the scope of their authority he is bound by.

Diehl vs. Ins. Co., 58 Pa. St., 443 ; Coles vs. Ins. Co., 18 Iowa, 426 ; Hackney vs. Ins. Co., *supra*.

One important consequence of this peculiar relationship is that the agent of a mutual company is more restricted in his powers, and assumes less responsibility in his dealings with the insured than in the case of a stock company. Thus, in the case of Hackney vs. Ins. Co., *supra*, representations of the agent regarding the limitations of the company's business were set up by the insured in defense, but the court declared that even false representations by the president would not affect the case. So, in Hale vs. Ins. Co. (6 Gray, 169), the by-laws required written consent of the president to subsequent insurance, and it was held that his verbal consent was not sufficient to waive the requirement. Again, in Brewer vs. Ins. Co. (14 Gray, 203), the by-laws made payment of premium a prerequisite to insurance, and it held that no officer of the company could waive the provision. In Smith vs. Ins. Co. (24 Pa. St., 320) the agent made statements in the application with the consent of the insured which were untrue, with the understanding that the facts should be made to correspond with the statement, and the court declared that in a mutual company the agent had no power to enter into such an agreement.

But the most important feature of mutual insurance is the liability which it imposes on the members. As in ordinary partnership, the members are liable for the debts of the company, and the extent of this liability is only limited by the provisions of the charter and their several contracts. Even though a member has lost all rights under his policy by a violation of its terms, this does not release him from liability for losses to others. In Commonwealth vs. Ins. Co. (5 Ins. Law Jour., 864) the policies had expired, but were subsequently renewed, the renewals being dated back, on the assurance of the secretary that the company was sound and strong. On the contrary, heavy losses had occurred in the interval before renewing, and the insured was held liable to assessment for their payment.

Not only are the members thus liable for losses among themselves, but where the company undertakes to do business also on the stock or non-participating plan they are in the same position as ordinary stockholders, and may be assessed for the payment of losses on such non-participating policies.

Schimpf vs. Ins.Co., 7 Ins. Law Jour., 663; Hayes vs. Ins. Co., 10 Ins. Law Jour., 507.

The questions which excite the most controversy in connection with mutual insurance are those respecting the rights and liabilities of the members on account of their premium-notes. In the ordinary mutual company the premium-note fulfills the twofold function of premium and capital. Sufficient cash only is required to meet current or expected demands, while a note subject to assessments is given for such sum as the charter or by-laws may prescribe.

Hayes vs. Ins. Co., 10 Ins. Law Jour., 507.

The general doctrine regarding such notes is that laid down in Commonwealth vs. Ins. Co. (3 Ins. Law Jour., 15), that a deposit-note given to a mutual company, aside from special stipulations, is just as completely within the control of the corporation as a cash premium, and may be assessed at the option of the company.

See, also, Nashua Ins. Co. vs. Moore, 4 Ins. Law Jour., 494, and cases there cited.

Assessments, however, must generally be equitable as between the members, and where limitations are prescribed in the liability, as for current losses, the fact of such losses must be shown. But the total destruction of the insured property will not release from liability to assessment until the insurance term is ended, nor will a forfeiture of his rights by the insured have this effect. It has even been disputed how far the surrender and cancellation or the expiration of the policy will release from liability in some cases.

Planters' Ins. Co. vs. Comfort, 4 Ins. Law Jour., 847, and cases there cited ; N. H. Ins. Co. vs. Rand, 4 Fost., 429 ; Sterling vs. Ins. Co., 32 Pa. St., 75 ; West Branch Ins. Co. vs. Smith, 5 Ins. Law Jour., 319.

It will thus be seen that the relations and responsibilities of a mutual policy-holder like those of an ordinary business partner essentially modify in many respects the powers and obligations of an agent of the corporation in dealings between the two. The general doctrine is, that the agent of a mutual company is more restricted in his powers than the agent of a stock company, both as to the terms and conditions of the contract itself, and the waiver of its provisions. In some States the courts hold these powers to be absolutely limited by the charter and by-laws. Any agreement in contravention of these, whether by officer or agent, is held invalid. The agent is treated as a representative of the applicant as well as of the company, and misstatements or omissions by him in the application are regarded as if done by the insured.

Jenkins vs. Ins. Co., 7 Gray, 370 ; Barrett vs. Ins. Co., 7 Cush., 175 ; Holmes vs. Ins. Co., 10 Met., 211 ; Smith vs. Ins. Co., 24 Penn. St., 320.

But in many of the States a more equitable view of the relations of the parties is taken, and the rights of the applicant who has not yet become a member, and may therefore be presumed ignorant of the rules of the company, and even of a member, are guarded as in ordinary stock insurance, in so far as a liberal construction of the charter and by-laws will permit. Thus, in Peck vs. Ins. Co. (22 Conn., 575), the consent of an agent to other insurance where the company knew he was in the habit of giving such consent, was held to be equivalent to the consent of the directors which was required by the charter. So, in Bebee vs. Ins. Co. (25 Conn., 51), the failure of the agent to communicate material facts stated to him by the applicant was held to be chargeable to the company, and not to the applicant.

Columbian Ins. Co. vs. Cooper, 50 Penn. St., 331 ; Woodbury Savings Bank vs. Ins. Co., 31 Conn., 517 ; Eilenberger vs. Ins. Co., 8 Ins. Law Jour., 822 ; Knox vs. Ins. Co., 10 Ins. Law Jour., 89.

INLAND UNDERWRITING.

Inland underwriting as practiced in this country combines many of the elements of both fire and marine insurance, and the law regulating it largely depends upon whether the issue pertains to the one branch or the other. Usage occupies a much more prominent place here than in ordinary fire-underwriting. The construction of the contract and the rights of the parties often depend upon the customs peculiar to our lake and river navigation, and a thorough understanding of these is of the first importance to the agent engaged in this branch, as well as a general knowledge of the principles regulating marine insurance. The transport policies usually employed in case of merchandise risks are of three kinds. One is an open policy on which shipments reported by the insured from time to time are indorsed by the agent at such rates as may in each case be agreed to, each indorsement being in effect a new insurance subject to the terms of the contract which the agent is free to make or not as he may elect. The second is a general contract between the company and the insured, in which the former undertakes to cover all transportation risks of a certain kind at prescribed rates of premium. The risks are by agreement reported at stated times, to be indorsed on the policy; but, unless this agreement is violated, the liability does not depend on the indorsement. The third class embraces those contracts which, as in ordinary fire insurance, are confined to specific risks agreed upon at the outset.

CLASSES OF POLICIES.

The courts draw an important distinction between policies like the ordinary fire-insurance contract, where the actual value of the subject or of the insured's interest is not stated, and those where a definite value is named in the contract itself. The former, popularly known as open policies, require the loss claimant to prove the existence and amount of his interest, while the latter fix the liability in case of loss by agreement, ment, and, except in case of fraud, no proof of value is required. It is manifest that a valued policy often furnishes strong temptation to fraud, and the character of the parties as well as the facts should be closely scrutinized in those cases where this form of contract is employed. The curse of what are known as valued-policy laws is that they thus convert the open policy into this form of contract, and even fraud is not recognized as a defense.

Sturm vs. Ins. Co., 5 Ins. Law Jour., 209; Bammessel vs. Ins. Co., 7 Ins. Law Jour., 767.

The year is the natural unit according to which policies are divided into long and short terms, and the rates are usually fixed on a commutation-scale diminishing proportionably with the duration of the contract. Hence arises the rule for cancellation according to which the premium charged as earned is the same as would have been the short rate charged for the same length of time. But the right to enforce this rule depends wholly on the stipulation to that effect in the policy, and the short rate is that which is customary in such cases.

CORRESPONDENCE BY MAIL.

Unless there is a special stipulation to that effect, the mere sending of a communication by mail is not a legal notification to the party of the contents of the communication until he receives it. The sender takes the risk of its miscarriage or failure to reach him. This is an important fact for agents to bear in mind in their correspondence with applicants and with the insured. But, on the other hand, so far as the sender is concerned, the communication is usually complete and beyond recall the moment it has been mailed, whether the party to whom it is addressed has actually received it or not. The moment an agent mails his acceptance of a proposition to insure, he closes the bargain. In Eames vs. Ins. Co. (6 Ins. Law Jour., 689) the general agent insisted upon a certain rate as conditional to the acceptance of a risk. The applicant wrote to the local agent agreeing to the rate, and the latter, in turn, wrote the general agent to the same effect, and requesting that a policy be sent, but directly after countermanded the order by telegram on account of the destruction of the building. It was held that the contract had been completed.

APPENDIX.

Page 17, last paragraph: "The contract is only complete when the insured has received the notice of its acceptance." In some States, as in the code of Georgia, mailing an acceptance completes the contract.

Page 47, fourth paragraph: "They [common carriers] cannot escape the consequence of such as are due to their own negligence." This is the general doctrine as laid down by the Supreme Courts of the United States, and most of the States. It has been held in New York, however, that a carrier may limit against loss by negligence.

Blair vs. R. R., 66 N. Y., 313, and cases cited.

Page 81, first paragraph: "It [cancellation] can be exercised only in strict compliance with the conditions." In Hollingsworth vs. Germania Ins. Co. (45 Geo., 294) the policy had been surrendered, and return premium directed to be paid to an agent of the insured, payment was delayed, but made and accepted after the loss, but before either party knew the fact. The policy was held to be in force.

INDEX.

92

www.ingramcontent.com/pod-product-compliance
Lightning Source LLC
Chambersburg PA
CBHW031441270326
41930CB00007B/819